Maryland Folklore and Folklife

Maryland
Folklore and Folklife

By GEORGE G. CAREY, Ph.D.

TIDEWATER PUBLISHERS
Centreville   Maryland

Standard Book Number 0—87033—154-X
Library of Congress Catalog Card Number: 71:142189

For

Betty and Jim

with thanks

Contents

Preface

This book had its inception in March, 1968. At that time, then Governor Agnew established a Commission to study Maryland's folklore and folk culture. The Commission's expressed purpose was to canvass the state to see what folklore activities were taking place and to assess the need for setting up a formal Archive of Maryland Folklore and Folklife. In March, 1970, after two full years of study, the Commission presented its findings to the General Assembly in the form of a final report. The report in turn became House Bill 1369 which came before the House late in the session and passed, but failed to get to the Senate before the General Assembly closed for the year. Another attempt to pass legislation will be made in 1971. The final report, published in a limited edition and distributed to all members of the General Assembly, included with the Commission's findings and recommendations, an *Introductory Guide to Maryland Folklore and Folklife* which I composed at that time for the Commission. This book is that *Guide* considerably enlarged and altered.

Even so slim a volume as this cannot be done without the help of a number of people and institutions. I am greatly indebted to the Commission whose constant encouragement spirited my writing, but more particularly to George Simpson, the Chairman of the Commission, whose helpful suggestions and unflagging interest in Maryland folk culture have been a keen inspiration throughout. I am also most grateful to Dr. Dorothy Howard who generously donated to the Maryland Folklore Archive at the University of Maryland a vast amount of folklore material gathered by her students at Frostburg State College over the last twenty years. Her donations have enabled me to make this volume much more representative of Maryland's folklore. Another folklorist, Henry Glassie, has also helped fill out the pages here. Without his advice, his photographs, and his drawings, this book would have lacked any section on material folk culture. To my students, and to all students in fact, who have contributed folklore collecting projects to the Maryland Folklore Archive, I owe more than a passing nod of thanks. Bereft of their labors, always carried out under the duress of a class assignment, Maryland would not have a folklore archive and this volume would still be a dream.

Further I am appreciative of grants from the American Philosophical Society, The American Council of Learned Societies, and the University of Maryland Research Board which enabled me to gather the material from the Eastern Shore of Maryland that appears in this book. Finally my typist, Connie Junghans, has been a faithful one and worked religiously under various difficulties; I thank her, and the English Department at the University of Maryland for lending me her assistance. And ultimately, my wife has made helpful suggestions, read manuscripts, been congenial when I have been ugly; she too is entitled to a deep genuflection of gratitude.

George G. Carey

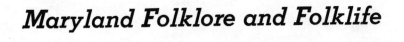

Maryland Folklore and Folklife

Maryland Folklore and Folklife
An Introduction

Terms and Definitions. Any consideration of Maryland folklore and folk culture must, by necessity, begin with some discussion of terms since the popular conception of folklore is all too frequently inaccurate and the popular notion about folk culture is no doubt nonexistent. Scholars argue feverishly over what is meant by folklore. The twenty-one definitions of the word appearing in the *Standard Dictionary of Folklore, Mythology, and Legend* bear some testimony to the variety of opinions which presently pervade the field. But for the scope of this brief survey, a reasonably coherent statement can be made that should clarify some of the material to be presented here as examples of Maryland folklore and folk culture.

Folklore is most easily discussed under two headings: folk and lore. What do we mean when we speak of a folk, or a folk group? Usually a folk group is defined by a number of factors, the most important of which is isolation. Though at present folklorists are becoming increasingly more interested in urban folk groups which isolate themselves within the confines of the city through religious or ethnic ties (for example, the Hasidic group in Brooklyn, New York), most collectors and compilers of folk material over the past fifty years have garnered rich harvests in geographically remote regions such as the Ozarks and the Southern Appalachians. One can easily see that small groups of people living in close communion outside the mainstream of progress and advancement have a tendency to conserve their patterns of life, their language, and their traditions. Old habits and customs remain the same, passed down from father to son to grandson in a long procession. And if the area in which this process takes place remains uncontaminated from outside sources, then the stream of tradition will stay pure. A mountain potter may mold his earthenware pitchers in the same way his great-grandfather did until someone brings a factory-made pitcher into the community. He may begin then to make some of his products after the more "modern" design, and thus the pure tradition has been corrupted.

1

There are other elements besides isolation which draw a folk group together. Occupation, for instance, binds people together. When all the people in a community make their living from the water, or in the mines, or on the farm, traditional beliefs and practices that emerge in those areas will derive much of their life force from the particular trade that fosters them. Religion, likewise, works to unify a group, particularly when it is as profoundly conservative as that of the old order Amish found several places in Maryland. When one adds to these factors such other ingredients as race, language, and, on a larger scale, nationality, it is not difficult to see that there are, in this large polyglot we term America, groups that can decidedly be set apart and called "folk."

To be sure, these folk groups as such are receding. The automobile has made America mobile. Highways cut back and forth across regions that were once barely accessible; bridges reach out to what were once virtually insular communities. Added to this, the mass media of television and radio and the cinema have made the folk modern. Old patterns of dress and speech fall to the "correct" mode as the television set becomes a necessary home appliance. Even the traditional life style is disturbed. The country store, once the breeding ground for every shred of "news" in the village, has now taken second place behind Walter Cronkite, and the store that used to remain open until ten or eleven at night so every wag might have his say, now buttons up nearer seven for lack of business.

Yet, despite this obvious drift towards modernization, folk groups still exist in Maryland. The old order Amish, as suggested, still pursue a traditional life style which dates back over several centuries. But one need not look for such obvious examples to witness folk culture. The Chesapeake Bay watermen provide an excellent example of a folk group bound together by their occupation, their religion, and their isolation. Their communities, stuck at the ends of long fingers of land or on islands, are virtually self-sufficient for the work that sustains them. Deal Island, for example, has its own sailmaker and boatbuilder, and the watermen themselves are proficient in manufacturing the smaller items necessary for their work. Or if one wished to go west in the state, he would find similar homogeneity among the miners, the lumbermen, or the farmers.

It is the lore which springs from these homogeneous groups, as well as the groups themselves, that most directly interests the folklorist. Lore, as the folklorist conceives of it, is traditional and orally transmitted.When it is active among a group, folklore does not appear on the pages of any book, but issues unconsciously from the lips of the people in a variety of forms. It becomes absorbed in an endless round of transmission: teller and listener, singer and audience, riddler and riddled. And with each retelling or resinging the item has a new birth, so to speak, as each individual raconteur or folksinger shapes the text to his own liking and adjusts it to suit his audience.

Folklore appears in a vast number of forms. To mention some of the more prominent: myths, legends, folktales, jokes, proverbs, riddles, chants, curses, oaths, tongue twisters, folk drama, folk belief and folk medicine, folksong, folk instrumental music, folk speech, children's games, counting-out rhymes, and jump-rope rhymes. Folklore also includes other forms that are not passed along orally, but are traditional. One thinks here of gestures, customs, folk dance, food recipes, and the more general subject of folklife itself.[1]

Traditionally carved gravestone motif in Deal Island
Cemetery depicts the waterman's life style.

Photographs not individually credited are courtesy of Henry H. Glassie.

The study of folk culture as a whole encompasses not only the oral traditions but also the collection and examination of the concrete items a homogeneous folk group may produce. If the oral traditions of that group give us what we might term "mentafacts," the arts and crafts and architecture of the same group provide us with "artifacts." The artifacts are frequently lumped together by folklorists and called, collectively, material culture. According to Henry Glassie, whose recent book, *Pattern in the Material Folk*

Culture of the Eastern United States,[2] is the first in this country to shed some light on the subject, material culture "embraces those segments of human learning which can be seen or touched" (p. 2). Glassie believes that in establishing an object of material culture as folk, it must first be examined in three different ways: in its form, construction, and function. He explains:

> Any object folk in construction is in itself at least partially folk; an object that was not folk when it was produced cannot become folk by usage or association, and a folk produced object does not lose its folk status when utilized in a non-folk manner. A guitar manufactured in a Kalamazoo factory is not folk even when played by a bluesman from the Mississippi Delta, for the object is not reinterpreted and then newly produced in a way the song the same man might have learned from a popular source might be. When a family moves from a one-story folk house into a modern two-story house and continues to live on only the ground floor, apportioning the space in the new house the way they did that in the old, they are using the house in a traditional way. . . . Conversely, when a suburban matron buys a homemade lard bucket at an antique shop and uses it for a planter, its use has no relation to its intended or traditional use, but provided it was traditional and non-popular when produced, it remains a folk bucket no matter how many zinnias she packs into it. (pp. 11-12)

Thus, for Glassie, the total examination of material culture would include a detailed and ordered description of field data, but not just with the goal of discovering the history of the dissemination of an item but with an eye to uncovering "its role in the culture of the producer and user . . . and what mental intricacies surround, support, and are reflected by its existence" (p. 16).

Collecting and Preserving Folklore and Material Folk Culture. To understand a national culture, particularly in this country, it is wisest to begin by learning something about the smaller cultural complexes that make up the whole. The folklorist contends that one of the most incisive methods for studying a folk group is to gather and examine the kinds of folklore that issue from it. By doing this, folklorists are, in effect, preserving material which the people of the group take for granted and invariably feel merits little or no attention. But what appears to the groups as a silly old story or a foolish saying, the trained folklorist recognizes as an international folktale or highly traditional belief. So he draws it into his collecting net and studies it to see what cultural adaptations have been implanted upon the item by that special group. Similarly, what the folk may think is just another crab shanty along the Bay, the student of material culture may quickly recognize as a traditional *croglofft,* a building type found along the coasts of the British Isles.

The author, second from left, talking to Captain Otis Evans, third from left, and other retired watermen on the "liar's bench" in Crisfield, Maryland. (Photo: A. Aubrey Bodine)

In collecting oral traditions such as songs, tales, beliefs, proverbs, and riddles, the folklorist is anxious to gather his material as close to the spoken word as possible. If he is honest, he will not tamper with his texts to make them literary, but will leave them with the same rough speech and bumpy grammar as he first heard them. To assure reliability of transmission, the folklorist frequently employs a tape recorder, taking down verbatim the words his informant utters. "On tape," writes Richard M. Dorson, ex-president of the American

Folklore Society and editor of *Buying the Wind,* "one hears the full-bodied, pristine narrative, replete with reflection and natural idiom; printed words cannot convey this vocal color. What the machine can do that the notebook cannot is to 'encircle' the text and capture conversational exchange and aside and revelation."[3]

Once gathered, the folklore must be housed and organized so it may be of some use to scholars and students bent on learning what traditions predominate in one region or another. The folklore archive serves this vital purpose. There are a number of these archives throughout the country in various stages of development, but perhaps the best known and most well established is the Archive of Folk Song at the Library of Congress. Recently, the Maryland Folklore Archive has been set up under the auspices of the English Department at the University of Maryland in College Park. At the present time, this archive holds more than four hundred collections covering almost every county in the state. Each collection includes, besides the texts themselves, as much peripheral information as the collector could secure. Such data as the name and background of the informant, the date and place collected, and the informant's own evaluation of the item's function is valuable for establishing the role folklore plays in a society. In other words, the text of a story collected and placed on a printed page has little substance unless we know whether or not it is still active in the oral tradition. Is the story just a memory, or is it told and retold and believed by the group? A proverb used in a family group as an educating device differs in value from one simply recalled by an old person as a "queer saying." A weather belief springs more fully to life when we realize that the man who possesses it trusts it much more than the murky predictions of the professional meteorologist. Clearly, by this added information the folklore itself is put into a broader perspective, and through the unconscious utterances that make up oral traditions we can begin to see more distinctly the cultural values of one group or another.

In broadening one's study and collection of a particular area to include aspects of material culture, several approaches are possible. One can venture forth with the express desire of acquiring actual artifacts for preservation, either traditional architectural types or traditional implements. But this procedure presents problems when it comes to housing and displaying the objects. A museum is needed. On the other hand, one can employ a more practical collecting technique by making use of a camera and measuring equipment. With these simple accoutrements, pictures can be snapped of artifacts and houses, barns, or outbuildings, while at the same time the objects can be measured so that drawings can be made later to complement the photographs. This sort of record can be easily filed and from it isographs can be constructed which reveal the location of these traditional objects and suggest their patterns of dissemination.

To date little collecting of this kind has been carried out in Maryland, and only flurries of activity have occurred in other states. The Ethnic Culture Survey in Pennsylvania has made bold attempts within the last several years to isolate and make available to the public the whereabouts of certain objects of material folk culture. At the University of Indiana in Bloomington moves are under way to construct an outdoor folk museum much along the same line as those found in the Scandinavian countries where the traditional and not the peculiar is emphasized. The fact is that many active museums in this country do indeed contain traditional folk items among their collections, but far too often these objects are crushed together with nontraditional curiosities, thus erroneously presenting the folk themselves as some sort of curious segment of the society which spends its time in quaint and picturesque ways.

Maryland as an Area for Folklore and Folklife Research. Until recently, the only activity which stimulated any collection of Maryland folklore occurred in 1899, when members of the Baltimore Folklore Society (later to become the Maryland Folklore Society and now, apparently, defunct) set about to gather traditions in the state using a contest as a format. The Society offered prizes for the largest collections of different types of folklore, and apparently the response was good for twenty-six years later the American Folklore Society published *Folk-Lore from Maryland* which drew from this material. The book, now obsolete, stands as the one endeavor to preserve Maryland's oral folk culture. And this fact is doubly lamentable when we realize that Maryland is bordered by three states, Pennsylvania, Virginia, and West Virginia, that have worked hard at collecting their folklore and have found their efforts richly rewarding.

For the student of folk cultures, Maryland furnishes a variety of groups that merit the systematic collection and study of field data. Not only is it a border state, thus containing a mingling of northern and southern language and traits, but within its confines one confronts urban ethnic groups and rural occupational groups, mountain settlements and maritime pockets, river people and farm workers. These groups and areas cry out for investigation.

Still the question arises, what earthly service can be performed by gathering, preserving, and studying the folk culture that these various groups display? Clearly, the more we know about any one group, be they Polish miners, Chesapeake Bay watermen, or urban groups, the more easily and comprehensively it can be explained to any other group. More complete knowledge of the smaller societies that go to make up the larger complex that is Maryland will reveal a rich diversity among groups and will surely unveil both an oral and material creativity among different people in the state, a creativity which to the present time has gone virtually unheralded. Moreover, accent upon a group will produce pride among the people themselves as their own arts and crafts become recognized. To accomplish such in-depth studies three major steps need to be taken:

1. Collection and examination of the group's folklore.
2. Collection and examination of the group's material culture.
3. Observations, recording, and study of methods used by the group for performing occupational or home pursuits.

Another aspect of folklore field research which swells the knowledge of one area or another is the collection and study of oral or folk history. This aspect can hardly be emphasized enough. Far too often historians place no value on historical fact that has been passed on by word of mouth. But, ironically, in certain locations this is the only history that is available since nothing has ever been recorded. A typical interview with a Crisfield resident reveals just the sort of material one might acquire:

Collector: What was it like around here back then?

Informant: Well, it's been thirty or thirty-five years ago that this whole river [the Annemessex] was lined with crab shanties.

Collector: So the trade's really fallen off, then?

Informant: Oh my, yes. And all the way down on that side over there by Mrs. Paul's Kitchen, all that marsh down there used to have shanties on it and there used to be upwards of a quarter of a million soft crabs go through here.

Collector: How much now?

Informant: Next to nothing compared. Lots of people have died and there is nobody to take their place, and no supplies if they did. They just don't do the business now simply because in the years before the automobiles they drew their supplies from all up and down the western shore of the Bay. But those people over there didn't have any facilities for shipping and most of those places didn't even have an ice plant or anything, and they would bring the fish here or send boats over to buy them their oysters and crabs.

Collector: Well, let's say forty years ago, were there many oyster-shucking houses?

Informant: Oh, twenty-five or so. Now there were three houses here; they would have three to four hundred shuckers, and they're all gone now. There are some small houses now, Christie's is about the biggest one and he's got about thirty-five shuckers. You can imagine the oysters that used to go out of here. There used to be mountains of oystershells. That metal plant over there that you see, that used to be used for grinding and burning oystershells. That was after they stopped building roads with them. . . .

Collector: Would you say the general life style is different here now?

Informant: Well, taking into consideration the general difference in the money situation, . . . there was a change in the people's way of life so far as most of them conveniences are concerned and all that. I would say this: there are a lot of them that don't have as much money as their parents did and their parents didn't have much, but it was a town where everybody had some. . . . Now the railroad, that come down from where the post office is and it came down on pilings to where the wharf was. Now all this land you see, all the way over from the marina to Paper Street—'cause that was literally built on paper—all that was made land. I don't care how deep you go down here you don't find nothing but oyster-shells. See, a man would start an oyster house and he'd build a wharf out and he'd build his oyster house; all these sanitary requirements they have now didn't exist then, and so he'd dump the shells through the trap door in the floor, and when that built up he'd use a wheel-barrow and by and by he'd make a place where someone else could make another oyster house. And Jersey Island, that's how that all got there.[4]

To be sure, the facts and figures in this man's account may not be wholly reliable, but it is one man's rendition of Crisfield's past that may be set against the record, if such record exists.

A more extreme case of the dearth of written historical information can be found on Smith Island in the middle of Chesapeake Bay. Here the only information that can be elicited is what people remember having heard from ancestors, and in certain instances family traditions harbor events that occurred during the War of 1812. An ex-Smith Islander recalled this bit of oral history.

My uncle told me this happened to my great, great-grandfather, and I suppose it's true. His name was William Evans and he was living on the Bay side of Smith Island, and at that time Smith Island was sparsely settled. They were scattered from Kedges Straits halfway to Tangiers. The old man had a farm and a herd of cattle and he thought enough of them as if they'd 've been Aberdeen Angus. But they were hide and horn mostly.

When the British left Baltimore after they got whipped [in 1814] they were becalmed off Smith Island and their provisions were about gone. They looked over through their binoculars and they could tell that there were cattle roaming around in the beach. So when the old man got up this morning, he looked down there and there was a long boat on the Bay shore and a bunch of bluecoats there around his cattle. Well, he saw the fire right away, so he grabbed his old walking stick and he got down there to the beach and he started waving that thing around, you know; so those men gathered him up, tied him and put him in the long boat, and took him aboard the boat.

Now this all happened when tobacco-chewing come in. The old man was a great chewer—grew his own tobacco. So he sat out there in the main cabin of the ship chewing his tobacco. But he didn't know where to spit. Oh, they had a plush carpet you would sink into. So by and by he found himself a corner and he spit into it. Here comes a little fella dressed up in white and he put down a big silver-looking thing, all bright and shiny. So after a little while the old man felt he had to spit again. He looked around—couldn't spit in that beautiful thing—so he found himself another corner and he let loose. And that fella run and grabbed that silver thing and put it in this corner. So this finally got on the old man's nerves and he said, 'If you don't take that *dahmn* thing out of my way, I'll spit right into it.'

'Oh, Captain Evans, that's just what we want you to do.'

'Well,' he says, 'good enough.' so he sat there. Said he had the greatest evening of his life. But later on it breezed up, so they went on down to Tangiers, 'cause they had a deep water harbor there. They went there for repairs before they went back to England. And they told Captain Evans—he had been as contrary as he could be—

'Mr. Evans, we're going to take you to England.'

He said, 'That's just what I want you to do, take me to England. I want to tell the *dahmn* queen just what kind of a bunch of cutthroats she sent over here, anyhow. You're no good.'

(And according to my uncle, my grandparents did hate the British. Oh yes, they called them *dahmn* Britishers, and they weren't cussing men as a rule. They were church-abiding men, but they'd use that word: *dahmn* Britishers.)

But anyhow, the day came that the British were all ready to sail back to England, and they changed their mind on grandpap. They said, 'Mr. Evans, you're too brave a man to keep in custody. We're going to send you back home.'

And so the man in charge put an officer over him and said, 'You take Mr. Evans back to Smith Island and you be sure to put him on dry land.' So when they got up there to Horse Hammock, the tide was down low and there was this sandbar going out there for one hundred yards or more from the shore. They said, 'Mr. Evans, you'll have to walk from here. This is as close as we can get.'

He said, 'I heard your commanding officer tell you: Put me on dry land! And you'd better do it or there's going to be trouble. I'll report you, certain.' So the four of them picked him up, one a-hold of each arm, and they carried him ashore and set him down on the grass. 'Now,' he said, 'you can go.' (ES 70-1)

To further emphasize the need for retaining oral history in the state, one could readily look to the variety of occupations, some dying, some already dead, that Maryland fostered. People who drew their livelihood from the C. and O. Canal, for instance, can still be found scattered along its shores, and reminiscences come easily to their lips if the right chord is struck by the collector. A Lonaconing woman recalled a violent incident on the canal that spawned a traditional song:

There was this man by the name of Johnny Howard who worked on a canal boat down at the C. and O. The captain got something against this young fellow and one day he came out on deck and he ran into Howard. The captain told Howard he demanded his life. At this, the young fellow picked up a spreader stick and killed the captain. There was this Negro standing close by and he saw the whole thing, but he told Howard he would take up for him at the trial. When the trial came, though, the Negro went against Howard.

So Johnny was proven guilty and was to be hung. Before this Howard wrote a song about the whole affair and sang it to the people before he got hung. The hillsides were covered with people watching Howard being punished. He was the first and last man ever hung in Cumberland. My mother used to sing that song, but I can't remember it all. It went something like this:

Captain walked out on deck
With a hatchet in his hand,
And he says to Johnny Howard,
"Your life I do demand."

And Johnny being a brave young man
Picked up the spreader stick
And laid the Captain out. . . .

The song was a lot longer than this. But you see, all the people sympathized with Johnny because he was such a nice looking young man. (H)

Other similar recollections of the Canal could easily be garnered and would certainly prove a viable historical footnote to that vanished way of life. Then too, the prolific memories of older watermen, miners, and lumbermen might actively be plumbed to gain some measure of the varied patterns of life that these professions nurtured in Maryland.

In the material that follows, it is hoped that some indication will be given to suggest what folklore and material culture resources lie untapped in Maryland. All the samples given in this book, with the exception of examples of material culture, are taken from the Maryland Folklore Archive at the University of Maryland at College Park. The material has been organized by genre rather than by cultural group simply because no major collections of any one group have been accomplished to date. If one notes a geographical discrepancy, again it is because some regions have been more assiduously collected than others.

Material Folk Culture
and Life Style

Many of the traditional patterns of life among folk groups have weathered the ocean passage. Yet one can readily see the inherent difficulties that immigrants have faced in sustaining their old way of life after moving to the new world. How does one perform the old customs and traditions in a new land? How does one perpetuate the old country ways among the younger generations when they grow up in an ever-modernizing society? Yet the old ways do persist, and frequently emerge in artistic expression as with the Polish dwellers in Baltimore who still paint the screens of their houses in bright pastel designs. Or traditional cooking habits may linger on as they do in Bethesda where the members of the Norwegian Women's Auxiliary frequently convene to trade recipes they knew as young girls in the old country. More deeply rooted, perhaps, are the folklife patterns followed by rural farmers of German descent in western Maryland. On small farms hogs were butchered according to a prescribed method:

> We usually butchered about six hogs a year. They weighed around 200 or 225 pounds and were about a year old. We always did this around Thanksgiving 'cause the meat would keep better in cold weather. Used to shoot the hog between the eyes with a twenty-two and one shot usually did the job. Then we'd slice the artery in the neck and allow all the blood to drain out for several minutes. Then we'd dip them in a large barrel of boiling water and that would scald all the hair and then we'd take a sharp knife and when the body cooled, scrape it clean. Then we let it cool overnight and the next day we cut the body lengthwise and cut off all the parts we needed. (70-5)

Around these German farms one might also find traditional methods for making butter and cottage cheese and apple butter, means for curing meat and tending livestock, as well as cooking and baking patterns which came over from the old country. A Garrett County woman learned this recipe for "filled noodles" from her immigrant mother:

13

First take some celery, about two onions, a little parsley, pepper and salt, about as much as you think. Stew the onions and celery in a little butter or oleo. Cut up bread (I use about two loaves), and then mix this with the celery and onions. (I never use the crust of the bread.) Over this pour the beaten eggs. Use as many eggs as you need to mix good with the dressing. For a big family take about three pounds of hamburger and fry it a little. Mix the dressing and the hamburger together. (The more meat you use, the better it is.) Make the noodles last. Cut them into squares. Don't let the noodles dry or they can't be folded around the dressing and pinched together. Cook the filled noodles in broth from a soup bone or boiling beef. (I always use about a dollar's worth of meat to cook to get the broth.) Cook the noodles about 15 or 20 minutes or a little longer than noodle soup. Be sure the broth is boiling when you put the noodles in. (H)

The same woman also cooked "Streusel Kuchen" or cinnamon cake in a traditional way:

Make sweet dough with eggs. Put the dough in a round pan. Smear butter over the top after the butter is softened or melted a little. Sprinkle sugar and cinnamon over the top and bake in a medium oven until they are brown on the top and around the sides. Eat it plain or spread butter upon it. (H)

Another traditional craft, long popular throughout the state in rural communities, was the art of quilt making. Different designs intrigued those who sewed the quilts and many patterns gained popularity and were passed on from one generation to another. Even the names of the quilting designs have a traditional ring about them: "Improved Nine Patch," "Rocky Road to California," "Cross and Crown," "Boston Commons," "Snowball," "Bow Tie," "Grandmother's Flower Garden." A woman from the western part of Maryland recalled the process of making a "crazy quilt pattern" in 1920.

The pattern for the patches was first cut from a piece of plain cotton material. Sometimes half-worn-out garments or sheets were used for this. Then the wool patches were sewn to this material. Two odd pieces of wool were laid right sides together on the pattern material and stitched to it. They were opened up and the other pieces were laid right side to right side and stretched. The uneven edges were trimmed to the shape of the original pattern and these "crazy" pieces were then stitched together.

The patches were all dark in color and all of the same quality material. The backing for the hap was dark blue cotton flannel.

The hap was filled with raw wool which my mother and grandmother carded. They first washed the wool in large tubs of water. When we were children we had to tramp the wool to squeeze the water through it. I didn't particularly enjoy this because the wool was so oily and I couldn't stand anything the least bit greasy when I was a child.

The colorful feather stitching between the patches was done with fine wool yarn and picked through to the underside to hold the wool in place. (H)

Also in the western part of the state, there is ample evidence that the traditional shivaree was frequently performed after marriages. Called bull-banding, the custom was known in the Frostburg region in the 1930's and the ritual invariably followed a set pattern as a female informant recalled:

In the section of Frostburg where I grew up, and among the people with whom I grew up, bull-banding was quite a ceremony for the newlyweds.

As soon as the couple were married, sometimes even as the couple left the church, a group of children and adults congregated for the purpose of bull-banding the bride and groom. To do this they came prepared to make all kinds of noises, such as blowing toy horns, pounding on old tins, until the groom treated the group. The groom was usually prepared for them and he had a lot of pennies which he threw out to them and let the crowd hunt them. If the weather was bad, he usually gave the leader enough money to take the crowd somewhere and buy them a treat. Mostly, the group consisted of children. (H)

In other regions in the western part of Maryland, the custom was termed "bellying" and could be carried out as late as two weeks after the couple had been married. In every case, however, the main object of the ritual was to have the bride and groom provide some sort of treat.

In looking for other traditional customs and occupational methods in Maryland, one might glance at the Chesapeake Bay watermen who, as descendants of settlers from the west coast of England, adapted traditional methods of fishing to fit their crabbing purposes. Long-lining, practiced in England for centuries, appears on the Eastern Shore as one way of catching hard crabs. Called trotlining by the

Traditional "I" house, one room deep and two rooms wide, found throughout the Eastern Shore and in southern Maryland.

watermen, this method requires a long length of line tied every ten feet with a piece of bait. The line is anchored at one end and payed out. As the line is wound back up on a winch, the crabs feeding on the bait are dipped into the boat with a net. Oyster dredging, too, dates back at least to sixteenth-century England, where we know that fishermen used a crude dredge made of bull's hide in which to secure their catch.

More tangible than traditional methodologies are the actual artifacts of material culture, and certainly the most easily witnessed of these is folk architecture. Traditional house types and outbuildings appear throughout Maryland. The "I" house (one room deep and two rooms wide) is English in derivation and crops up along the eastern seaboard and especially on Maryland's Eastern Shore. Similarly, in pockets near Thurmont and in areas of Garrett County, one encounters typical log houses built in the nineteenth century and frequently enlarged later. The design reveals an interesting collusion of cultures, as the log frame house is often Pennsylvania German in construction and Irish or Welsh in form. It is much the same sort of building as the log houses found in the southern mountain region of the country.

Log house with later addition, near Thurmont in Frederick County. The building was constructed with traditional v-notched joints.

The Pennsylvania Barn, or Bank Barn, as it is sometimes called, also combines traits of German and English traditions. Built on two levels with space for livestock below and hay above, these barns contain a prominent forebay and one notices that this barn type is highly popular in Lancaster County in Pennsylvania but is less widespread in Harford and Carroll Counties directly south of Lancaster County, a fact which confirms the well-documented movements of the settler from northeast to southwest. Once more the combination of German and English traditions can be witnessed in this kind of barn. Many of them stand out due to the pierced-brick patterns on their sides, a fancy way for allowing ventilation and securing the structure against spontaneous combustion. Similar pierced brickwork appears on buildings in parts of south central England, while the barn form itself springs from German influences.

With other outbuildings we find a dissemination pattern analogous to that of the Bank Barn. Stone springhouses with overhanging roofs dot the landscape around Chester County, Pennsylvania. They virtually fail to appear in Maryland counties directly south of Chester, but one finds them as outbuildings on farms in Frederick County. Tobacco barns appear in southeastern Maryland and Virginia, influenced in design by the old English hay barn or loft. This older form was simply transposed internally to meet the need for storing tobacco, while the outside structure remained basically the same.

Tobacco barn near Piscataway in Prince George's County with handhewn beams and stalls for cattle in the rear.

One way to observe the sweep of a folk group's life style is to examine a traditional building type to see just how it functioned and how the artifacts it contained served the person who dwelled in the building. One need not walk far along an Eastern Shore marsh before spying a crab shanty. Common and uninteresting as these shacks may seem to local inhabitants, many of the designs are part of a rich tradition, descending from the *croglofft*[5] found all along the southwest coast of England, original home of many early settlers of the Eastern Shore. A small crab shanty on the Annemessex River north of Crisfield fits this description.

Pennsylvania German barn in Frederick County. Note semi-enclosed forebay at bottom and English-influenced pierced brick ventilation design at right.

Stone springhouse in Frederick County, similar to outbuildings in Chester County, Pennsylvania. Handhewn beams support roof overhang.

Eastern Shore crab shanty near Crisfield. Interior is identical to *croglofft* found along the southwest coast of England.

Rocking chair handmade of barrel slats and found in Crisfield shanty is not necessarily traditional but indicative of the waterman's creative values which relate to function.

The waterman, whoever he was, built his shanty out over the water and alongside it he cut a short slip to draw his boat up and tie it. He constructed his building simply, with a bedroom, a pantry, and a living room, and the structure stood just over one story high. Outside he built himself a porch facing the water, and then (using barrel slats) fashioned a rocking chair to sit in on summer evenings and catch the cool breeze blowing in from the southwest, and perhaps whittle a boat model.

The waterman designed the interior of his shanty so that only the main room went all the way to the eaves of the building, while the bedroom and pantry were enclosed, forming a loft which he reached by ladder. In the main room he kept a tool bench, replete with tools

Cutaway sketch showing interior design of Eastern Shore crab shanty. Bedroom door is at right. Loft above for storage of waterman's implements was reached by a ladder. (Drawing: Henry H. Glassie)

for working on his boats and repairing his fishing gear. In the loft over the bedroom, he stored the traditional instruments of his trade.

On a given morning, the waterman climbs to the loft and pulls down his eel gig, an object resembling Neptune's spear, and used traditionally since prehistoric times for taking eels or spearing fish.

Eel gig traditionally made and used on the Eastern
Shore, in New England, and old England.

Eel pots made of oak and used on the Eastern Shore, in New
England, and throughout the British Isles.

On eel days, he also hauls down his eel pots, cylindrical items woven with oaken strips, which trap the eels on the bottom. But it is doubtful that this man would be aware that this same sort of eel pot had been used by his ancestors in England for several centuries, or that his nearer neighbors in New England still use them.

In oyster season, the waterman reaches for his tongs or his nippers depending on whether he wishes to go after his catch in deep or shoal water. In crab season, he grabs his crab scrape, or his dip net, and he is sure to throw into his boat a "tow smack" which he will tow behind his craft and fill with soft crabs, not realizing that the same object had been used in England for generations for keeping fish fresh.

Nippers, short tongs used for taking oysters in shallow water.

On a fall day too rough for oyster tonging, the waterman climbs to his loft and hauls down the bag of hand-hewn duck decoys that he carved the way his father taught him. He throws them into his boat and departs the shanty for a day of gunning in the marshes. And the boat he made, of course, with its strange ram, or reverse sheer bow,

Tow smack, used on the Eastern Shore for keeping soft crabs fresh for market.

Traditionally handmade duck decoy carved by Captain Ira Hudson of the lower Eastern Shore. (Courtesy: Mrs. Alton E. Hughes)

is modelled after the Spanish-American battleships he had admired cruising the Bay in earlier years.

What one finds here, then, in this composite picture, is the microcosm of an entire life style spelled out in terms of one building filled with folk implements, traditionally made and traditionally used. This waterman, like so many others, spun out his day-to-day existence probably unaware that his methods had been tried and worked successfully for years and years.

In his Eastern Shore shanty he lived in the present, but ever so much in the past. He crab-netted or scraped, trotlined or tonged, depending on the season and the day. And after his workday on the water was over, he doubtless returned to his shack in the evening, sat in his homemade rocking chair, and shared tales he had heard from his forebears with anyone patient enough to listen.

Folklore

Folktales. Folktales in Maryland appear in a number of different guises. The people who tell the stories seldom differentiate among them. The raconteur may readily lump a legend, a jest, and an anecdote together under the category of a "good yarn." Or he may term a tall tale simply a "lie," quite unaware of its traditional nature. But to the folklorist, all tales can be distinguished under such headings as märchen (or fairy tales), belief tales, legends, tall tales, jests (or jokes), fables, anecdotes, and so forth.

What students have noticed about storytelling along the eastern seaboard is that the mode is predominantly anecdotal. Such would appear the case for Maryland. The telescoping of time in this age hardly permits the extended ramification of the type of folktale the Grimm brothers collected at the outset of the last century. Though many of these wonder tales did make the ocean passage and have been collected in isolated regions of the Appalachians, this kind of story, it seems, is infrequently passed along orally in Maryland. But on occasion one will surface, as did this truncated version of "Cinderella" collected in Salisbury:

> Lady had two daughters and adopted Cinderella. That make three. So the king had a big dance that night and at that dance the king was supposed to find a wife. The king had one golden slipper and whichever lady that slipper fit, that would be the king's wife.
>
> So this lady dressed her two daughters the best she could in pearls and diamonds because she knew her daughters would look beautiful and put poor Cinderella in the dutch oven and locked her in.
>
> As the king asked for a dance with the slipper in his hand, whoever he danced with was supposed to fit the slipper to her feet. So the lady said, 'Mr. King, here are my two beautiful daughters. I know it will fit either one, so take my daughter to be your wife.'

So the king tried the slipper on both girls' feet and neither one could wear it. So he said, 'Madame, dear lady, I'm sorry neither one of your daughters can be my wife because they cannot wear my golden shoes.'

And at that time poor Cinderella began to sing in the oven: 'You can repair your feet, and you can cut off your toe, but the owner of that slipper is in the oven.'

So the king said, 'Madame, I heard someone singing. May I see the lady singing?'

She said, 'Oh, Mr. King, don't listen to that dirty little girl. She's just a nuisance when good men come around. My daughter is the girl to wear that golden slipper.'

The king said, 'How can that be when it doesn't fit her foot?'

The lady said, 'Oh, Mr. King, we can cut off the toes so it will fit. She must be your wife.'

The king said, 'Madame, it just wouldn't work.'

At that moment, poor Cinderella began to sing again, 'You can repair your feet, you can repair your toes, but the owner of that slipper is in the oven.'

So at that Mr. King walked around to the great big brick oven and poor Cinderella jumped out of the oven. The lady said, 'Mr. King, don't look at that little dirty girl.'

Mr. King said, 'I'll give her a chance.' So at that Mr. King gave her some soap and water to clean her and as he presents the golden slipper to Cinderella she slipped it right on her feet. Perfect fit. So she became the wife of the king. (ES 68-2)

More elaborate is this tale from Garrett County, clearly German in tradition. The tale offers an interesting composite of several international folktale types known throughout Europe. It combines a numbskull story with the well-known tale of "Dungbeatle" in which the princess is made to laugh. To this composite, the storyteller has appended a scatological ending.

There was this German couple and they had a son and he wasn't too smart. They had just come over to America and they lived in the woods. One day the son was sent out to chop some wood. He was chopping the wood and he found a needle and he put that needle on his arm and then put the wood on top of it. By the time he got home he'd lost the needle. He told his mother about it.

She said, 'Hans, you shouldn't have done that, you should have stuck it in your coat lapel to bring it home. You're never going to get the American ways.'

He was out again and found a shovel plow. He remembered what his mother told him and he stuck the shovel plow into his coat and tore his lapel. When he got home he told his mother about it.

She said, 'Hans, you shouldn't have done that, you should have carried it on your back to bring it home. You're never going to get the American ways.'

He was out again and he found a donkey. He remembered what his mother said and he carried that donkey on his back for half a mile. When he got home he told his mother about it.

'Hans, you you shouldn't have done that. You should have rode it home. You're never going to get the American ways.'

So the next time he was out he saw a buck deer. He climbed the tree and the leaves began to fall and Hans fell too. He landed on the buck backwards. He held onto its tail and yelled, 'T'other way, t'other way.'

Now back in the hills there lived a king and his daughter who had never smiled and the king said whoever made her smile could marry her. She was sitting on the porch reading a book when Hans came riding by on the buck backwards yelling, 'T'other way.' The princess had never seen anything so funny in her life and she began to laugh. She sent some of her subjects to catch the buck with the man riding on it backwards. They caught Hans and brought him back to the princess and the king.

The king went into the room while Hans was getting dressed for the wedding. He said, 'What do you want for your wedding feast?'

Hans thought and he said, 'I want bean soup.'

After the wedding everyone went to the wedding feast of bean soup. Hans kept eating and eating and eating. You get pretty hungry after riding a buck deer, especially backwards. Well, Hans finally finished and he'd eaten about two bushels of bean soup.

They finally got to the bedroom. He was in his finest and she was in her silk nightgown. He laid down and said, 'Oh, I gotta get up.'

'There's a pot under the bed,' she said.

Hans overflowed the pot under the bed and finally returned to the bed. A few minutes later: 'Oh, I gotta get up.'

This time he went to the wash basin, but he still wasn't through. He kept looking around until he found the king's boot and still he had to go.

'Go out behind the haystack,' the princess said.

Well, he filled up that area, so he looked around until he found himself a corncob to use as a stopper. He went back into the bedroom and climbed over the princess to get into bed. A straw scratched her that he'd brought in from the haystack and she pulled the stopper and Hans went all over her. She yelled and the king came running and slipped on the mess on the floor.

'I'm gonna kill you,' said the king.

Hans ran out of the house and under a tree and ran smack-dab into a giant beehive. Just as he got into the beehive, two men came 'round looking for beehives. They found the one Hans was in and said, 'This is great, feel how heavy it is.'

So they both carried it off and pretty soon it started dripping and one said to the other, 'This is a good hive. Just look at the honey pouring out of it. (Little did they know that Hans was just feeling more of that bean soup.)

'Let's taste it and see if it's good honey,' said one of the men. So they did and it wasn't.

Hans was shipped back to Germany on the next boat. (H)

Another widely known tale type is the story of "The Golden Arm," frequently spun out at camp gatherings as a scare story. Two versions of this tale, the first from Cumberland and the second from Princess Anne, reveal the alterations a story can acquire as it moves through the process of oral tradition.

One day these people moved into a haunted house, but they didn't know it was haunted. That night they went to bed, and at twelve o'clock they heard a voice saying, 'I'm on the first step; I'm on the second step; I'm on the third step; I'm on the fourth step; I'm on the ninth step; I'm on the tenth step; I'm in the hall; I'm at your door; I'm at your dresser; I'm by your bed; I'VE GOT YOU!' (H)

Once upon a time there were two boys, and John's mother sent him to the store after some liver. He met up with his neighbor down the road and so he got him to go along to the store with him. So they shot marbles all afternoon until it was dark, and then John forgot what his mother sent him to the store for and he said, 'I'm going to have to run back home and see what my mother sent me after so I can get it.'

On the way back the little boy who was with John said, 'John, I know what your mother sent you for. She sent you for liver.'

So they kept on until they happened to see a dead man and he was on the side of the road. Well, they knew that the store was closed by this time, and so this other boy said, 'John, I'll tell you what to do. Take the liver out of that dead man and carry it home.'

So John decided that's what he would do and he took the liver out of the dead man and headed for home. John had farther to go than his friend, and when his friend left him John went on by himself, and pretty soon he heard this voice behind him and it said, 'John, I want my liver.'

So John began to run and he ran and he ran until he got almost home and when he slowed up, he heard that voice: 'John, I want my liver.' He ran on and when he got home his parents had gone to bed and John went right into the house and right behind him came this noise, 'John, I want my liver; I'm in the doorway behind you and I want my liver.'

John ran upstairs and got into bed. There were ten steps on the stairs. And the voice said, 'John, I'm on the fifth step and I want my liver; John, I'm on the ninth step and I want my liver; John, I'm on the tenth step and I want my liver; John, I'm in your room, AND I'VE GOT YOU AND I WANT MY LIVER. (ES. 68-48)

Equally familiar to Maryland raconteurs is the tale, "Dividing Up the Souls." In European versions of the tale the characters duped are often churchmen, but in this version from Princess Anne, as in most American versions of the tale, the listeners are not definitely specified.

One time there these two boys stole a pack of walnuts and then wanted to divide them up and the only place they could find where they wouldn't be bothered was the graveyard. So they went in there and they started to count them out. 'You take this one, I'll take that one; you take this one, I'll take that one.'

And pretty soon a man come along down the road and he heard something going on in the graveyard: 'You take this one, I'll take that one.' And he ran as hard as he could to the first neighbor's house and he said, 'The Lord and the devil are down in the graveyard dividing up the dead and I want you to go down there.'

Of course, that fella didn't believe him but he went along anyway. They got down there to the graveyard gate and they stopped and they heard the two counting them off: 'You take this one, I'll take that one; and those two we dropped down by the gate, you take one and I'll take the other.' Those two men ran away from there just as fast as they could go. (ES 68-48)

ii

Much more profuse in Maryland tale-telling than the märchen is the legend. Richard M. Dorson observes:

Legends deal with persons, places, and events. Because they purport to be historical and factual, they must be associated in the mind of the community with some known individual, geographical landmark, or particular episode. Any or all members of a given social group will have heard of the tradition and can recall it in brief or elaborate form. This indeed is one of the main tests of a legend, that it be known to a number of people united by their area of residence or occupation or nationality or faith.[6]

One might add to this the fact that legends, unlike most märchen, are recounted to be believed. What occurs in the transmission process of a legend is that a small bit of oral tradition (known to the folklorist as a "motif") which has been passed around by word of mouth becomes attached to a particular person or place where the situation is applicable. Often, in the case of a legend that draws on the supernatural, the story becomes the people's attempt to rationalize an inexplicable event: a strange light, an odd noise, a headless apparition, an ineradicable bloodstain. Perhaps the last, the ineradicable bloodstain, is as ubiquitous as any motif that finds its way into Maryland legendry. We find it surfacing in this account from St. Mary's County:

Down around here there's an old plantation called Mulberry Field. The owner of this place came home one time and found another man in bed with his wife. A fight started between the two men and the plantation owner killed the lover. They took him off to jail but because of the circumstances of the crime, he only got a two-year sentence.

After the owner had served his sentence he came back to his plantation. He found a bloodstain on the floor, right where he killed that other man. He tried to clean it up, but he couldn't get if off. So he had them come in and take the floorboards up and put new ones down. Those new boards were only in there one night and that stain appeared on them too. So then this man tried to cover up the stain with a rug, but the stain came right through the rug.

They say he left that place and never came back, and that those stains are right there today. (67-6)

But if we begin to examine the state, we discover the motif appearing in a number of different guises. West of Frostburg, at the foot of Meadow Mountain, a Union soldier was reputedly brutally murdered in a home where he had taken lodging. When he tried to escape he left the bloody print of his hand on the heavy wooden paneling of the front door. Despite all attempts to remove it, the stain remained there as clear as the night it had been left, until the house burned after the turn of the century. So, too, do the folk attempt to rationalize the mysterious bloodstain on a Thurmont gravestone with a legend:

There's a tombstone around here that is said to bleed at certain times of the year. There was this man who was in a terrible accident. He was taken for dead and buried. They say around here—I didn't know him or his folks; I had friends that did—that he wasn't really dead when they buried him and that's why the stone bleeds. They say that he tried to scratch his way out of the casket and that he broke his fingernails and wore his fingers down to the bone and bled to death finally. They say that stone bleeds on the day he died. I don't know, but they say there're dark stains on that stone all the time. (67-24)

Often old homes will radiate legends. Strange incidents and inexplicable appearances fostered this tale in Frederick, Maryland:

There is a huge old house in Frederick which at one time many years ago was the most beautiful estate in the county. It is old now and condemned and it's been vacant for over thirty years. Yet no one will tear it down. It is said that the old woman who lived in the house was a very old person. She loved that old home so much that she would never leave it. She lived there with her daughter for many years. One night the old woman had a heart attack, but before she would let her daughter take her to the hospital, she wanted to put on her brand new pair of shoes. So the daughter put the new shoes on her and placed the old worn-out shoes on the hearth of the fireplace in the living room. The old woman died that night. After the funeral, the daughter went back to the house to clear it out so that she could sell it. She saw her mother's shoes setting by the fireplace and tried to pick them up but they were stuck. A lot of people have tried to pull those shoes off but no one has ever been able to budge them. To this day those old shoes are still stuck on the hearth of that fireplace. People say that each night they see a figure walking into that house, yet all the doors and windows are boarded up. They see a light go on in the living room, but there is no electricity in the house at all. Everyone says it's the old woman as she said she'd never leave that house. I have heard this story over and over from many people who really believe it. (69-7)

Other legends focus on bridges where strange sights occur, as in this Harford County story:

When I was a child in Harford County everybody knew about the ghost of Peddler's Run. I was afraid to pass by there in an automobile. I'd hide my head to keep from looking.

It seems that in the old days, a long time ago, peddlers would come through that country on foot, carrying their wares in a pack. A headless body was found by the run and buried under some rocks nearby. They couldn't find the head, so they buried the body without it.

After that, people reported seeing a headless figure walking about the area and pushing a long stick into the ground. They said it was the peddler's ghost looking for his head. I never saw him. Like I said—I was too afraid to look. (68-56)

The average impression of folklore is that it exists predominantly in rural settings. One all too often envisions the old-timer with his corncob pipe and his jug of whiskey spinning yarns on the porch or around the stove of the local country store. But just as frequently, story and song, jest and game appear on the streets of the city and are carried on in traditions with the same persistence that they are in the country. To wit, the legendary cycle of tales surrounding the statue of "Black Aggie" located at one time in a Baltimore cemetery. One Timonium woman recalled:

> The statue of Black Aggie is in the Reisterstown cemetery and it's a reproduction of the one in Washington. The story connected with the one in Baltimore doesn't relate to the one in Washington, the original. The curse of Black Aggie is by a woman who was originally buried under it and who was supposed to have been a witch. Teenagers and superstitious people have taken to playing games or trying to thwart the superstitions involved. The story concerned is that this supposed witch cursed the statue and if you run around it three times and jump in her lap you will die in two weeks. There have been people recently who have had parties around the area, trying to mass-jump into the lap to see if they would die. (68-32)

But a Sykesville, Maryland, girl held a different opinion:

> In 1913, a young Negro girl who was sixteen was said to have been raped by a neighborhood gang and the people who lived around there collected some money and bought a tombstone and they called the statue 'Black Aggie.' I guess she died from the assault and the people must have liked her and felt bad about what happened. Anyway, she was buried in the cemetery off Reisterstown Road near Baltimore and the statue was put over her grave. They say that any virgin placed in the outstretched arms of Black Aggie will lose her virginity in twenty-four hours. (69-143)

Place-name legends also flourish throughout the state. Actually many of the more colorful stories deal with places that seldom appear on Esso road maps or geodetic survey charts. It is doubtful one would know, for instance, that he was driving along "Ghost Light Road" near Hebron, Maryland, unless he happened to ask a resident. And if the traveler were curious enough to inquire further he would find a variety of supernatural tales to explain the naming of the road. There are, moreover, a number of towns in the state whose names also give rise to imaginative tales. Accident, Maryland, according to one informant, acquired its name when an Indian borrowed a white man's axe to split wood. After he returned it badly chipped, he explained: "Axe, he dent."

To be sure, many of the folk etymologies are erroneous and stem more from a whimsical imagination than any grounding in fact. Yet they are the local inhabitants' explanations of the nomenclature and must be considered in the total study of the place-name history. For example, we know for a fact that Rockawalkin on the Eastern Shore developed from an Indian name, but most residents will tell you a story akin to this:

> One time around here there used to be an old man called Rock. He didn't do very much walking. Everywhere he went, he either rode a bicycle or drove a horse and buggy. One hot day there was a group sitting under a shade tree at the end of a long lane. One gentleman looked up and said, 'Look, here comes old Rock a-walkin'.' From then on that's what this place has been called. (ES 70-1)

From some place-names several legends emerge. Two different accounts depict the naming of Silver Spring.

> Whoever was the owner of the Lee property had a daughter, and they were out riding one day. His daughter was apparently a good horsewoman and went ahead of her father on her horse and as she was riding, the horse's hoof fell into a hole and threw her. When her father came up they discovered that the horse had fallen into a spring and when they saw it, it reminded them of silver. There was just one spring so they called it Silver Spring—not Springs, like in Florida. (69-127)

> Silver Spring got its name from the mica spring under the big acorn. It was a very hot summer day and Montgomery Blair had dismounted from his horse. Then the horse ran away. When Blair found him he was drinking at this spring which was silvery from the mica. So Blair called it Silver Spring. (69-127)

People as well as places germinated legends. A local personality, known in his community for some remarkable trait, be it strength or cunning or endurance or even supernatural powers, gathers around him during his lifetime a cycle of tales, some true, some fabricated. After his death, these feats still linger on in the anecdotes of the

local people. With time, the existing tales are considerably em-
broidered while other traditional stories become attached to the cycle
and before long a legendary figure of local stature but incredible
proportions emerges.

Not surprisingly, men who contracted with the devil gained this
sort of legendary notoriety. But unlike Faust, whose demonic alliance
brought him knowledge, figures in Maryland folk narratives sold their
souls for money or the power to work more productively than
anyone else. A Crisfield wizard named Skidmore went to an
appointed place in the woods for nine consecutive nights, whereupon
the devil appeared and an agreement was reached. From that day on,
Skidmore possessed a miraculous skill for cutting wood.

> They used to say around here that you'd be going in the
> woods in the early morning where he'd been working and
> you'd hear more than a dozen axes going hard as they
> could. And when you got up to him, you didn't see a soul
> but Skidmore and he'd be sitting on a stump. But if you
> looked around you'd see any number of cords of wood,
> more than one hundred cord cut that very morning. But as
> soon as you'd leave, you'd hear all those axes going again.
> (ES 70-1)

A man in the western part of the state near Frostburg also signed
with the devil; his contract enabled him to dig more coal than
anyone else.

> There was this fella 'round here. He had quite a reputa-
> tion, but I don't remember his name. They said that the
> devil worked with him in the mines. He'd go down in the
> mines when nobody else was in there and the first thing
> you know, there'd be a trip of coal on the line. They
> couldn't figure out how he done it, that coal was dug in so
> short a period of time. So some of them went in there to
> watch him, and directly they heard car wheels going and
> coal falling. They got worried and got out of there as quick
> as they could. When they asked him how he done it, he
> said the devil helped him. (H)

Belief in the occult likewise gave rise to witchcraft, and frequently
a witch became sufficiently well-known in a community to spawn a
spate of tales which lived on after her death. A Crisfield man recalled
one such woman who lived on the Eastern Shore of Virginia.

Now this woman I'm gonna tell you about lived down in Hunting Creek on the Eastern Shore of Virginia. My grandmother said this was a true story. There was this waterman and his name was Jim Cannon and one day he was tying up at the wharf and this woman who they said was a witch came down there just as he come in. Well, he had two baskets of hard 'jimmie' crabs and a basket of fish. She came up to him and she wanted that mess of fish. He said, 'Lady, to tell the truth, I just got enough for myself, but I got some hard crabs. Do you want them?' They were good lively ones, too.

Well, she put her hand down in that mess of crabs and they all dropped their claws and every one of them died. She put a spell on those crabs. So he got mad when he saw he'd lost all that money and he started for home, and she said, 'You'll be sorry of this. Won't give me that mess of fish.'

That night he went down to the local store and on his way home she overtook him and turned him into a beast of burden of some sort, a horse or mule or something, and she rode him all the way down to Cape Charles, some hundred miles through the marsh and brambles and bushes just to get some fish which he'd refused to give her. So when he come home he was all cut up with briars and everything and all out of breath so that his wife called the doctor.

The next day he got a gun shell, and he took all the shot out and he put in some small pieces of silver and he wadded it back in and he drawed a picture of that old woman as best he could and he put that on the wall and shot at it. And a day or so after that she got sick and died, and they say where the silver hit that picture is where it hit her—in the legs, breast, and stomach. (ES 70-1)

More prominent in rural areas, perhaps, are local figures who gain stature among their neighbors because of sheer physical strength. Their deeds become legendary in the community and are told and retold long after the hero dies. "Lickin' " Billy Bradshaw of Smith Island gained the reputation of bully of the island. He heisted 196-pound barrels of flour with one hand, held broom handles at arm's length while islanders loaded the handles with weights until they broke. He challenged all comers to fights and seldom lost. Once, when attacked by three Virginia boys, he struck one and knocked him out; he picked up the second one and threw him ten feet, and the third boy ran. But when he went by, "Lickin' " Bill kicked at him and his big brogan shoe came off, hit the side of the store and split a weather-boarding plank. Another strong man from Fairmount named George Davey likewise provided feats of strength that tested credulity.

> They used to go to Baltimore in them little pungies and bugeyes. And one time when George Davey got his oysters out, there was a man come up there and put his bowsplit [sic] across his deck so he couldn't drop out. George Davey told him if he'd slack his lines, he could get out of his way and allow him to come in alongside of the dock. This man said he weren't going to slack nary a line until he'd passed every one of his oysters across Davey's deck. George Davey walked right over there, took that bowsplit in his arms, like that, lift-up of her and down, and broke it off even with the knightheads. And out he went. Now by all accounts, he was a man. (ES 70-1)

At times tall-tale motifs become attached to local heroes and expand the story cycle notably. West Virginia yielded Timothy Corn, a recognized hunter and woodsman during the early settlement of that region, but stories about him still linger in Garrett County.

> While deer hunting Tim came to a circular mountain and climbed to the top. He got there and jumped the biggest deer he ever seen. It ran 'round the mountain so fast that all he could see was a blur. After thinking how to get a shot at it, Tim wondered why a bullet wouldn't travel in a circle too. So he bent the barrel and fired his old rifle. The shot went 'round fifteen times before it caught the deer. That old shot had a bead of sweat on it as big as a walnut. (H)

Local characters likewise have a way of attracting traditional stories. Two short tales told on a man named Henry from Pompey's Smash are also pinned on personalities in neighboring towns.

> One day Mr. Henry was shingling his roof, when all of a sudden there was a terrible clatter and a bang, and he fell off the roof. His wife was pretty scared and she ran out of the house and helped pick him up... asked him if he was hurt, you know. Mr. Henry looked himself over and said, 'No, I'm not hurt; I was just coming down for some more shingles.' (H)

On another occasion (this was after his wife died), she was laid out in the house. Well, Mr. Cook, who was the Frostburg undertaker, was there and he was offering his condolences, you know. So Mr. Henry shook his head and said, 'Oh yes, it's pretty bad, but it could have been worse.'

'What do you mean, "it could have been worse."?'

'Well, it could have been me!' (H)

Another traditional tale is hung on a local character from Eckhart, Maryland.

It was the custom for men who like their beer to come to Frostburg and get what was called a 'dutchman'; that was a keg of beer containing about four gallons. They carried it on their backs. Well, one time Boggy Eisentrout of Eckhart came to Frostburg and got his dutchman and started home sometime after dark, and he was a little the worse for the amount of beer he'd drunk. To get home he had to go through the Eckhart cemetery. It was pretty dark and Boggy fell into an open grave that had just been dug. 'Course, he couldn't get out. Well, he sat there and drank a lot of that beer and after a while he fell asleep. When he woke up he noticed his surroundings and he jumped up and cried, 'Great Jupiter, it's Resurrection Day and I'm the first one up!' (H)

In Klondyke, Maryland, the local character was a man named Ike Morgan. Morgan ran a local saloon and grocery store called The House of Morgan, and the tale cycle that framed Morgan as a local legend turned primarily on his witty responses. Once, when in Frostburg, someone asked him how business was in Klondyke. "Business," said Ike, "what business? Why things are so slow over there the creek only runs three times a week." Another time Ike came home drunk one winter night and fell through the ice into the creek. A neighbor came by and heard Ike hollering, "Hey Mag, will you put on some more covers?" Not surprisingly, a story widely told on various characters throughout the state also got pinned on Ike.

One time Ike had been drinking quite a lot and his wife, Maggie, thought she ought to do something to slow him down. So she got her brother and the two of them decided to work something out.

A couple of nights later, Ike was coming home and he was pretty drunk. All of a sudden his brother-in-law

stepped out from a bush beside the roadside with a white
sheet over his head and shouted, 'Oh! oh! oh! I'm the
devil, I'm the devil.'

'Good,' said Ike, 'I'm glad to know you. Come on up to
the house; I married your sister.' (H)

As is the process with most material that circulates in oral
tradition, legends are constantly being recast in modern guise and
related by young people. Stories about girls whose fancy hairdos
spawn cockroaches (sometimes black-widow spiders) often cast
aspersion on local hairdressers, just as a recent rash of tales drew
unfavorable attention to Klein's sweater department as being the
place where baby cobra snakes were hatched. To say that the youth
of today have no folklore is utter nonsense. They have their own
cycle of legendary accounts merely shaped in current language and
image. Take, for instance, this modern legend told throughout the
country by teenagers and usually associated with the local "parking"
place.

Here is a version from Leonardtown:

There was a couple who were parked out on a lonely
road down near the river. The girl and her boy ran out of
gas or something happened to their car. The boy left to go
get help. The girl fell asleep on the seat and one time she
woke up during the night and she thought she heard
scratching on the roof of the car, but she didn't think
anything of it. She thought it was just some twigs and since
she didn't have a watch, she didn't have any idea what time
it was. She thought maybe he had just left. The next thing
she knows, it's morning and there's a police officer near her
car. He woke her up and said, 'Miss, please get out of the
car and walk to the police car but don't look back.' But as
she was walking to the police car, her curiosity got the best
of her and she turned around and looked back. And
hanging from the tree, by his feet, over the car, was her
boyfriend and he looked like he'd been slit. His clothes
were all in rags and he was bleeding. He was dead. What
she heard during the night were his fingernails scratching on
the roof of the car. (69-55)

Equally modern and widespread in oral tradition is the story of the
"death car," invariably recounted as true though no informant ever
admits to having seen the car himself. The Silver Spring man who
provided this version maintained that his tale was common knowledge
in the area.

You know that car dealer out on University Boulevard? Its specialty is repossessed cars. Well, they say that they repossessed this red Corvette a few years ago. The owner had been murdered and hidden in the trunk. Well, this car dealer cleaned up the car, repainted it and recarpeted the trunk and about a week later they sold that car to some guy. But he returned the car after a week, said there was a bad smell in it that he couldn't get rid of. This happened a couple of more times with other people who bought the car, and now that dealer is stuck with the car. I think its going price is something like $100. But it serves them right; that place is a big clip joint, anyway. I hope they never sell that car. (69-133)

iii

No less than the legend, the tall tale has had a long and active existence in Maryland storytelling. Unlike the legend which appears at home in both the country and the city, the tall tale thrives best in rural settings. Though not indigenous to the United States, this oral story form is generally associated with the westward expansion when land was lush, soil amazingly fertile, and game abundant. Tall-tale tellers invariably recall their yarns with a straight face, drawing the innocent listener along in all seriousness to the end, when he realizes that he has been completely duped. A Marion raconteur tacked a widely disseminated tall tale to a local man there.

One time old Jack Ball said he went out in the thicket near his home to cut some wood, and after he had cut it up and was just getting it loaded on his wagon, it started to rain. So he ran up right quick and took his horse by the bridle and led him up to the house and tied him to a post near the barn and ran into the house. When he got into the house he looked out and the wagon was still down there by the woods. That rawhide had stretched that far. He said to himself, 'Damn if I'm gonna go down there and get that tonight; I'll wait till tomorrow when the weather is better.' But he slept late the next morning and when he woke up the sun had been out a while, and when he got to the barn there was that wagon hooked right up to the horses. The sun had dried out that rawhide and drawn that wagon right up there to the barn. (ES 68-34)

Characteristically, human traits such as miserliness or indolence get stretched into tall tales, as in this well-known version told on a nameless Frostburg lazy man.

> Now they tell this about the laziest man in town. No one knew his name and if they did they didn't mention it. This fella was so lazy he wouldn't do nothing, and it got so bad that he wouldn't even eat. Some of the men in town thought it was high time something was done about this man and so they decided to bury him alive. So they put him in this old wagon and started for the cemetery.
>
> They were riding along and they passed this farmer working in the field and he asked them where they were going. They said they were taking the laziest man in town to the cemetery to bury him alive because he was just too lazy to live.
>
> Well, this farmer, he offered to give the lazy man a bushel of corn rather than see him be buried alive. When the lazy man heard that, he raised his head about an inch and looked over the edge of the wagon and said, 'Is it shelled?'
>
> 'No,' says the farmer.
>
> So that lazy fella motioned and said, 'Drive on.' (H)

Other tall tales foster common annoyances such as snakes and mosquitoes that become larger and more annoying than in real life. According to several people on Deal Island, the mosquitoes there bite with such consequences that a man needs a blood transfusion right after he is bitten. And from Garrett County comes this traditional story:

> There were these two fellas going through town and when it got dark they started to look for a place to spend the night. Pretty soon they found this house and went into the bedroom. Well, it was a pretty warm night and the mosquitoes were terrific. These two fellas covered themselves over with covers and after a while one of them looked out and he saw a lightning bug, and he'd never seen one of them before, so he said to his partner, 'Jim, it's no use—we might as well give up; they're hunting us with lanterns now.' (H)

A good number of tall tales evolve from the lubricated imaginations of fishermen and hunters. One story, widely circulated in nineteenth-century sporting sheets like the *Yankee Blade* and the *Spirit of the Times*, finds new life in the oral tradition of the Cumberland region:

> Now I've always heard that country moonshine was powerful around here, but this tale will bear me out. It seems that Mrs. Morison's uncle and her father went fishing one time and as always they carried their jug along. They came to this water moccasin who was just about ready to swallow this frog. So Mrs. Morison's father took a forked stick and clamped it down over the snake's head and took the frog away 'cause he wanted to use it for bait.
>
> Well, that snake looked so darn downhearted that they gave him a drink of moonshine, and off he went. So they went on with their fishing and about an hour later one of them felt a tug on the leg. He looked down and there was that snake back with another frog. All I can say is, that must have been awful good whiskey. (H)

Hunting yarns frequently rely on the preposterous ability of a good hunting dog, dead or alive. According to a Crisfield raconteur:

> There was this fella down here one time and he had a wonderful rabbit dog. Well, this dog died and he decided that he had to do something to remember him by so he had him skinned and made himself a pair of gloves out of that dog's hide. One time he was out in the forest working, and he pulled his gloves off and laid them on this stump and set down to eat his lunch. All of a sudden this rabbit run out of the underbrush and those two gloves jumped off of that stump and grabbed that rabbit and choked him to death. (ES 70-1)

Another internationally known tall tale, usually entitled "The Magnificent Hunt," appears in a variety of forms told by different raconteurs. Here a Garrett County yarn-spinner uncorks an extended version of the tale and gives it authenticity by placing himself in the lead role.

> I've been hunting going on fifty years now, but none of my experiences can equal the shot I made with that old muzzle-loader the very last time I shot it. I was out by myself and I only had enough powder to load one shot.
>
> Well, I climbed out of the lowlands through the brush and laurel to higher land which was supposed to be loaded

with game of all kinds. (God, what a time I had getting that six-foot muzzle-loader through that underbrush.) But I didn't have too long until I came to some game. I looked up and there was a big buck with antlers like a white oak tree staring me right in the face. But the funny thing was, just at the same moment I noticed a big old black bear looking at me from a berry patch and a flock of turkeys squawking over my head, and I looked to my left and there was a groundhog about the size of a spring pig scrambling out of his hole.

Well, I thought there was more choice meat on the deer than anything else, so I ups and let him have it. That thundering gun blew up right in my face. The shot hit the deer, the stock struck the groundhog, the barrel blew off and killed the bear and the ramrod caught those turkeys around the legs and held them tight.

Just about that time, I saw some honey running out of a hole in a tree—I've never been one to let anything go to waste—so I went to get a handful of leaves to stop the honey, and when I did, I caught a rabbit by the ears.

Well, I loaded the game on my back and started for home which was about four miles away. I didn't think I'd have too much trouble, but that oak tree that I was dragging behind me got rather heavy just as I reached the creek about one-quarter of a mile from home. But anyway, I jumped into the creek with my hip boot flaps up, and that tree tied to my waist. The current got hold of me and just took me downstream. But I didn't get too mad, 'cause when I got out on the other side, I put my hand in my boots and I found I had about a bushel of bass in there, from about one to two feet.

So I got up on the bank and started for home. Now, I don't know if it was the weight of the nine turkeys in my pants' pockets or the rotten old thread that my Ma sewed my suspender buttons on with, but while I was walking through the meadow to the house one of those buttons flew off and killed a pheasant flying overhead. (H)

iv

Another very common type of folk narrative found throughout Maryland is the belief tale. These stories usually spring to the lips of raconteurs in the form of a personal anecdote which simply elaborates a traditional folk belief. For instance, the oft-cited waterman's belief that it is bad luck to take black luggage aboard ship finds its way into a short tale recalled by an Eastern Shoreman.

> Now there used to be a man by the name of Ed Bussell and he was fishing a big boat. It was a steamer, and he couldn't catch no fish. So he stepped up on deck one time and said, 'Every man that's got a black satchel down there in that forepeak, bring it on deck.' So they brought them on deck. 'Now,' he said, 'I'll give you a dollar apiece to throw them overboard, every one of them.' And that was what they did. He said, 'There ain't a man in the world can catch fish with all them black things down there in the forepeak.' Now when he did that, they commenced to catch some fish. (ES 70-1)

Belief tales often surface as death tokens employing such common motifs as the death knocks. This tale, collected in western Maryland in 1948, recounted an incident that occurred seventy years before.

> When this took place, I was much too young to remember anything about it. But I've heard my mother and father tell it so many times, I can tell just what happened.
>
> Both my parents were very religious people, and I know this is an actual happening, because I've heard them declare it true. It was on a cold winter night around 1880. All the family were asleep, when all of a sudden everybody heard this knock, loud and clear. My father got out of bed and went to answer the door. But there was no one at the front door or at the back door either.
>
> The knock had waked up all the children. It was just so plain that everybody thought someone else had rapped on the wall of their room. But they found that no one had ever knocked. Everybody was all excited, but my father persuaded them all to go back to bed and go to sleep. But my mother and father couldn't go to sleep; they were too worried.
>
> Well, about two hours later, they found their fears were right. A second knock came at the door. This time there was a man there and he told them that my brother Lloyd had been killed just two hours before in a train accident. (H)

Quite occasionally the token takes the form of the deceased himself as in this account from Frostburg.

Now this was in the winter of 1926. I was only a year old. At that time we lived up on the Pope place. Mom and Pop was in the kitchen of our little log house and Mom seen someone come up the lane with a lantern. Pop saw it too. And the next thing Mom knowed she saw grandpap's face in the window. Pop went to let him in, but there was nobody there. They didn't see any tracks or anything.

About an hour later, Uncle George come and said that grandpap had died at suppertime. That was an hour before; just when they saw the face. Now that was a token of some sort. (H)

At times belief tales derive from inexplicable events and because of their sensational nature, they endure in the oral tradition of a small group. A tale from the mining region of western Maryland and one from Harford County suggest the variety one may encounter when collecting this sort of narrative.

My husband's one grandfather, Hugh Atkinson, worked in the mines in England. One day he was working alone in one of the little headings that lead to the main tunnel. He thought he heard someone calling to him. The voice just said, 'Hugh.'

He waited for a little while but he didn't hear anything so he went back to work. A little while later he heard it again—'Hugh.' This time he answered and went to the mouth of the heading to see if he could see anyone. But no one answered and he didn't hear anything.

He had just started to work again, when he heard that same voice say, 'Hugh, Hugh, come here.' It was much more insistent this time. So he went to the main tunnel where most of the men were and asked around if any one of them had called him. They all said they hadn't called him, so he just decided that they were playing some kind of a joke on him and he went back to where he'd been working. When he got back there, he saw that while he'd been gone the digging had caved in. If he hadn't left and followed that voice, he'd of been buried sure. (H)

There was a man who worked at a mill and the man would pay awful wages and he wouldn't pay without you stayed a month. Nobody could stay a month. There'd be a witch come at them at night. So one man went there and he stayed. One day before his time was out, why that witch come. He had his hand axe with him. He caught that cat by the paw and chopped the paw off and he got a woman's hand. He kept the hand and she came and got it later. She begged for it. He got his money. Said he wasn't afraid. Now this story was told to me by my father. (68-39)

V

The jest and the joke, as storytelling forms, likewise persist in Maryland. The jest, an older name for joke, is constantly being readapted and fitted into modern guise. These tales usually circulate about a certain group, schoolteachers, numbskulls, or preachers. The Pat and Mike cycle of tales so widely known in this country furnish good examples of the jest. Or from western Maryland we get another series of numbskull tales told on "an old Dutchman." For instance:

Then there's this other Dutchman tale I've picked up at one time or other. It's supposed to have happened locally, but I don't know where.

An old Dutchman came to a hotel one night and asked for a room. They gave him one on the third floor. After he'd been in bed for some time he heard someone shout, 'Fire, fire.'

So he jumped out of bed in total confusion and gathered up all his bedclothes and articles of clothing and carried them all downstairs. Then he ran back to his room and threw all the furniture out of the window. Then he put his pants on backwards and jumped out the window. So the rescue squad was down there and they caught him in their net and helped him to his feet.

They said, 'Are you hurt, old man?'

The old Dutchman looked himself all over, noticed his pants and said, 'No, I'm not hurt, but I believe I got a hell of a twist.' (H)

In highly religious communities on the lower Eastern Shore, the parson comes in for some humorous knocks in the narrative jests that flourish there. From Lawsonia comes this story told as true:

Now this really happened down here. There had been a change of preachers here, and this new man he come into that institution of learning, the country store. What you couldn't learn there wasn't worth learning. Well, there was this old fella laying 'round there after a day's work and this preacher was trying to get acquainted with his future flock and he walked into the store and greeted this old man who was laying on the bench chewing tobacco.

'Good evening. I'm your new preacher here and I'm trying to get acquainted with the members of the church.' The old guy never noticed him. 'I notice the soil seems to be fertile around here. Looks like you could raise most anything on it. What crop do you raise most of?'

The old fella looked at him and spit again, 'Well, the only thing I knowed them to raise around here was a lot of hell and they get about 500 good crops of that every year.' (ES 70-1)

The modern joke is so profuse in its many diversions and perversions that it almost defies classification, though folklorists are making bold attempts to distinguish between types. One type which has recently come under increasing scrutiny is the "ethnic slur." That is a story in which one group casts aspersion upon another under the disguise of humor. During World War II, the answer to the question, "What is the shortest list in the world?" was always given as "Italian war heroes." But after the recent Arab-Israeli war, Jewish jokesters pinned the list on "Arab war heroes." Similarly does an older story get a new life at the hands of a splendid Jewish raconteur from Silver Spring:

> And oh, yes, then there's the one that Gloria thinks is very cute. This comes out of the six-day Israeli War. There's a whole company of Arabs marching along in the desert. And there in the distance they spot one lonely Jew. And they send six men out to get him. An hour passes. Nothing. So they send fifteen men out to see what happened to the six. An hour passes. Nothing. They now send out fifty men to see what happened to the fifteen. Couple of hours pass. Here comes one guy staggering back, bloody, beat up, uniform torn in half off of him. And he comes staggering back to the commander and says, 'Go back, go back; it's a trap. There's two of them.' (69-91)

Another type of joke that has recently been studied is the shaggy-dog story which in a way seems to spoof the whole story-telling process. Instead of providing the conventional humorous ending, the raconteur winds through an extended tale before finishing with a *non sequitur* punch line, as in this college student's version which turns on an advertising slogan.

Long ago in merry old England there was a king who wasn't too merry. His castle was being besieged by a bunch of barbarians. He knew his people could not ward off the attack themselves. He thought, 'If only I could get help from a neighboring king.' The kings in those days would help each other out like that. So the king sent out one of his knights to take a message to another king. The only problem was that the knight had to cross a bridgé that was guarded by two huge yellow hands. These hands would grab anyone who would try to cross that bridge.

So the knight went out, but he never made it across that bridge. The king then sent out two more knights, but the yellow hands got them too. Then one of the king's page boys came up and pleaded to go. But the king said, 'No.' After the page boy pleaded and pleaded, the king finally relented because he was desperate. They just had to have help. When the page came to the bridge, he walked right across. The yellow fingers tried to get him but they couldn't 'cause he was too small.

And the moral of that story is: 'Let your pages do the walking through the yellow fingers.' (70-8)

Folksong. Traditional folksong has long thrived in Maryland. This we know. Unfortunately, along with other types of folklore, songs have been spottily collected over the years, and published only in rare instances. A remarkable collection of 113 songs in the Maryland Folklore Archives, all gathered from one family in Anne Arundel County, suggests a healthy singing tradition from that region.

On the Eastern Shore the white singing and fiddling tradition has given way to the Methodist religion, but among Eastern Shore blacks traditional religious songs still are heard, not only in the country churches but also to a diminished degree in the crab houses of Crisfield. Limited collecting in western Maryland also reveals that a good strain of traditional music was passed along in that area, but since virtually no work by folklorists has been carried out in the northeast or central portions of the state, it is difficult to speculate what folksongs, if any, are known there.

I think there is no doubt that traditional folksongs can be found anywhere in Maryland if the collector is avid enough. Perhaps the richness and pervasiveness of this type of folk entertainment may not exist in the same pristine form in Maryland as it did in the Southern Appalachians when the English collector, Cecil Sharp, canvassed that region in the first quarter of the century. But these few examples from the state seem to indicate that some Marylanders did sing and that they did not learn all their songs from records or the radio.

A fine example of folksong from eastern Maryland is this version of "Sir Patrick Spens," a ballad with antecedents both in England and Scotland. This version was collected from a man in Virginia who claimed to have learned it from his mother in Queen Anne's County around 1915, and his mother, in turn, had learned it from her mother:

Sir Patrick Spens[7]

The king sat in Dum-ferm-line town Drink-ing the blood-red wine, "Oh,
where'll I find a skee-ly skip-per to sail this ship of mine!"

1. The king sat in Dumfermline town
   Drinking the blood-red wine
   "Oh, where'll I get a skeely skipper
   To sail this ship of mine?"

2. Then up and spoke an eldern knight
   Sat at the king's right knee,
   "Sir Patrick Spens's the best skipper
   That ever did sail the sea."

3. The king had penned a braid letter
   And sealed it with his hand;
   And sent it to Sir Patrick Spens,
   Was walking on the strand.

4. "To Noraway, Sir Patrick,
   To Noraway o'er the foam,
   Queen Margaret's lass of Noraway
   'Tis thou must bring her home."

5. The first word that Sir Patrick read
   He laughed loud and high;
   The next word that Sir Patrick read
   A tear blinded his eye.

6. "Oh, who has done this cruel thing,
    To tell the king of me,
    To send me out this time o' the year
    To sail upon the sea?

7. "But be it wind, or be it sleet
    My ship must sail the foam,
    To seek the king of Noraway
    And bring his daughter home.

8. "So hoist the sails, my bonny boys all,
    With all the speed ye may,
    For we must clear the channel bar
    Before the cock crows day."

9. They hoist the sails, they cleared the bar.
    For ice-bound Noraway;
    But had not anchored scarce a week
    Before the lords did say:

10. "Ye Scotchmen spend our good king's gold,
    And all our white money."
    "Ye lie, ye lie," Sir Patrick cried,
    "Ye bawdy dogs, ye lie."

11. "Make ready, made ready, my good men all,
    For I will sail ere morn."
    "O prythee, sire," his pretty page cried,
    "I fear a sudden storm."

12. "For yetereen I saw the new moon
    With the old moon in her arms;
    And I am faint and sore afraid
    That our ship will come to harm."

13. They had not sailed a league, a league—
    A league but scarcely three,
    When the north wind grew black and the winds blew wild,
    And the waves champed angrily.

14. The anchors broke, the topmast fell,
    It was such a deadly storm;
    And then the waves came over the ship
    Till all her sides were torn.

15. "Go fetch me a bolt of the silken cloth
    And another of flaxen twine,
    And wrap them into my good ship's sides
    To let not the sea come in."

16. They fetched up a bolt of silken cloth,
    And another of flaxen twine,
    And wrapped them into the good ship's sides
    But still the sea came in.

17. Oh, very loath were the good Scotch lords
    To wet their cork heeled shoon,
    But long ere the doleful day was done
    They wet their hats aboon.

18. Oh, long, long may the ladies sit
    With their feathers in their hands;
    Before they see Sir Patrick Spens
    Come sailing to the strand.

19. And long, long may the ladies sit
    With their gold combs in their hair,
    A-waiting their own true loves
    For them they'll see no more.

20. For forty miles off Aberdeen,
    It's fifty fathoms deep;
    And there lies good Sir Patrick Spens
    With the Scotch lords at his feet.

Much more widely sung throughout the United States was the ballad, "Pearl Bryan," that depicted the maudlin fate of a young girl murdered by her two lovers. The events suggested in this Garrett County version actually occurred in January, 1896, in Kentucky, when Scott Jackson and Alonso Wallings murdered Pearl and cut off her head. They were executed for the crime 14 months later.

Pearl Bryan

Down in a lone-ly val-ley where the fairest flow-ers bloom
There's where poor Pearl Bry-an Lies a mold-er-ing in her tomb

1. Down in a lonely valley,
    Where the fairest flowers bloom,
    There's where poor Pearl Bryan,
    Lies a-mouldering in her tomb.

2. She died not broken-hearted
    Nor by disease she fell.
    One moment's parting took her,
    From the ones she loved so well.

3. One night the moon was shining,
    The stars were shining too.
    Down to Pearl Bryan's dwelling,
    Jackson and Wallings flew.

4. "Come Pearl," they said, "let's wander,
    All through the woods so gay,
    While roaming we will ponder
    Upon our wedding day."

5. The woods were dark and dreary,
    Pearl was afraid to stay.
    Says she, "I am so weary,
    Let us retrace our way."

6. "Retrace your way, no never,
    For in these woods you're doomed.
    So bid farewell forever,
    To the loved ones all at home."

7. Down, down she knelt before them
    And pleaded for her life,
    While through her snowy white bosom,
    They plunged the fatal knife.

8. "Dear Jackson, I'll forgive you,"
    She said with dying breath.
    "You know I n'er deceived you,"
    And closed her eyes in death.

9. With banners floating o'er her,
    The wind made try with sound.
    A stranger found poor Pearl,
    Cold, headless on the ground.

10. These two young men were taken,
    And in a dungeon laid.
    Death was the promised sentence,
    For murdering this poor maid. (H)

"Floyd Collins" was a later song which issued from another tragedy occurring in Kentucky in 1925. It first appeared as a broadside ballad but soon found acceptance with the folk and passed into oral circulation. This rather standard version was collected from a St. Mary's County woman in 1968.

Floyd Collins

1. Come all you young people
   And listen while I tell
   The fate of Floyd Collins,
   A lad we all knew well.
   His face was fair and handsome;
   His heart was true and brave,
   So his body now lies sleeping
   In a lonely sandstone cave.

2. How sad, how sad, the story,
   It fills our eyes with tears.
   Its memories too must linger
   For many, many years.
   A broken-hearted father
   Who tried his life to save,
   But his body now lies sleeping
   In a lonely sandstone cave.

3. "Fair mother, don't be weary,
   Fair father, don't be sad.
   I'll tell you all my troubles
   And of the awful dream I had.
   I dreamed I was a prisoner,
   My life I could not save.
   I cried, 'Oh must I perish
   Within this silent cave?' "

4. His mother often told him,
   If out my son don't go,
   It would leave us broken-hearted
   If this should happen so."
   But Floyd would not listen
   To the oft advice she gave,
   So his body now lies sleeping
   In a lonely sandstone cave.

5. His father often told him
   Of follies and disaster,
   And told him of the awful danger
   And of the awful risk.
   But Floyd would not listen
   To the oft advice he gave,
   So his body now lies sleeping
   In a lonely sandstone cave.

6. Oh how the news did travel,
   Oh how the news did go.
   It traveled through the papers
   And on the radio.
   A rescue party gathered,
   They tried his life to save,
   But his body now lies sleeping
   In a lonely sandstone cave.

7. The rescue party labored,
   They worked both night and day
   To move the mighty barrier
   That stood within the way.
   To rescue Floyd Collins,
   This was their battle cry.
   "We'll never, no we'll never
   Let Floyd Collins die."

8. But on the fatal morning
   The sun rose in the sky.
   The workers still were busy,
   We'll save him by and by.
   But oh how sad the ending,
   His life could not be saved,
   So his body now lies sleeping
   In a lonely sandstone cave.

9. Young people all take warning
   Of Floyd Collins' fate
   And get right to your making [sic]
   Before it is too late.
   It may not be a sand cave
   In which you meet your tomb,
   But at the bar of judgment
   We too must meet our doom. (69-44)

Railroad songs also find Maryland singers. One Cumberland woman recalled a version of "The Wreck of the Old '97" from members of her family who had worked on the railroad for years. The actual wreck occurred near Danville, Virginia, in 1903, when Joseph A. Broady drove his train off the Stillhouse Trestle at an excessive speed. When they found him in the wreck, it is believed that his hand was not "on the throttle," as the song states, but on the brake.

The Wreck of the Old '97

1. They give him his orders at Montrose, Virginia,
   Saying, "Steve, you're way behind time.
   This is not '38, but it's old '97;
   You must pull her in Centre on time."

2. He looked around to Jack, the greasy fireman,
   "Just shovel in a little more coal;
   And when we cross that White Oak Mountain
   You can watch old '97 roll."

3. It's a mighty rough road from Lynchburg to Danville
   And a line of a three-mile grade,
   It was on this grade that he lost his average,
   You can see what a jump he made.

4. He was going down grade making ninety miles an hour,
   When the whistle blew into a scream;
   He was found in the wreck with his hand on the throttle,
   And was scalded to death by the steam.

5. Now, ladies, you must take warning
   From this time now and on,
   Never speak harsh words to your true-loving husband,
   He may leave you and never return. (68-27)

Equally interesting is a version of "The Wreck of the C. and O." known by a western Maryland woman who said the song had been in her family for three generations. Her conversation about the song drew attention to Hutton, Maryland, mentioned in verse #2 as a place near where the accident occurred. Actually, George Allen was killed on October 23, 1890, when his engine hit a landslide and overturned near Hinton, West Virginia, but oral tradition has merely localized the event for effectiveness.

The Wreck of the C. and O.

1. Along came the F. F. E.,
   The fastest on the line,
   Running o'er the C. and O.,
   With a "yu-yu" on the line,
   There to receive an order,
   Twenty minutes behind the time.

2. And when he got to Hutton,
   The engineer was there,
   Georgie Allen was his name,
   With bright and golden hair.
   His partner Jack Dixon
   Was standing by his side,
   There to receive the order,
   "In the cabin you must ride."

3. George's mother came to him
   With a basket on her arm,
   Saying, "Oh my darling son,
   Be careful how you run.
   For many a daring life's been lost
   When trying to gain lost time,
   But if you guide your engine right,
   You'll get there just on time."

4. "Mother I know your advice is good,
   And later I'll take heed.
   I mean to run Old 94
   The fastest ever seen.
   I mean to run Old 94
   With speed unknown to all,
   And when I whistle for the big tunnel,
   I know they'll hear my call."

5. George he called to his partner, Jack,
   "Just a little more extra steam,
   I mean to run Old 94 the fastest ever seen.
   I mean to run Old 94
   With a speed unknown to all,
   And when I whistle for the stockyard gates,
   They'll surely hear my call."

6. George he called to his partner, Jack,
   "A rock ahead I see.
   I know that death is waiting
   To grab both you and me.
   So from this cabin you must fly,
   Your darling life to save,
   For I want you to be an engineer,
   When I'm sleeping in my grave."

7. So up the road she darted,
   And on the rock she crashed,
   Upside-down the engine turned
   And on a rock she smashed.
   Georgie on the firebox lay,
   And the flames around him flew,
   He said, "I'm glad I'm an engineer
   To die on the C. and O."

8. The doctor came to Georgie's side,
   "My boy you must be still,
   And if it be God's good will,
   He'll give you strength to live."
   "Oh no, doctor, I want to die,
   I want to die so free,
   I want to die by the engine I love,
   One hundred and ninety-three." [sic]

9. His last word,
   "Jesus lover of my soul,
   Let me to thy bosom fly,
   While the nearer waters flow,
   While the temple is still high." [sic]
   George was a Christian boy,
   A noble lad was he,
   The last words that he uttered,
   Were, "Nearer my God to Thee." (H)

Versions of three other very traditional songs found in Maryland offer some further idea of the nature of folksinging within the state.

Gospels of Libby

1. In the Gospels of Libby a fair damsel did dwell;
   For wit and for beauty, there was none could excel;
   A young man who courted her to be his dear,
   And him by his trade was a ship's carpenter.

2. Her blushes more sweet than the roses in June
   To answer, "Sweet William, to wed I'm too young;
   I will offer to venture, and therefore to bear
   That I cannot marry a ship's carpenter.

3. "For in times of war, you see they will go
   And leave wives and children oppressed with woe;
   And the prettiest of women that ever was born,
   When she gets married, her beauty's all gone."

4. "Well, if you will meet me when tomorrow comes,
   License shall be got and all things shall be done";
   With the sweetest of kisses they parted that night;
   She went the next morning to meet him by light.

5. He said, "My charming Mary, you must go with me,
   Before we get married, a friend for to see";
   He led her through groves and through valleys so deep;
   At last charming Mary began for to weep.

6. "I fancy, sweet William, you're leading me astray,
   A purpose my innocent life to betray";
   "That is true, and what more can you say,
   The grave being dug and the spade standing by."

7. "Is that my bride's bed and this I shall have?"
   "This is your bride's bed and there you shall lie,
   For I've been this long night a-digging your grave";
   Poor harmless creature when she heard him say so
   The tears down her cheeks like a fountain did flow.

8. Her hands white as lilies for sorrow she rung,
   Crying for mercy and "What have I done?
   O spare my sweet infant, lest my soul be astray;
   Must I in my bloom so be hurried away?"

9. There's no time to dispute and no time to stand;
   He quickly took a sharp knife in his hand;
   He pierced her fair breast while the blood it did flow;
   And into her grave her fair body did throw.

10. He covered her up and returned to his home,
    Left nothing at the grave but the small birds to mourn;
    And on board of Benford, he entered straight away,
    His full intentions bound out for the sea.

11. Charlie Stuart, being a young man with courage so bold,
    That night as he was going down in the dark hole,
    He espied this fair damsel; unto him she appeared,
    And she in her arms held a baby so fair.

12. Being merry in drink, he went to her embrace,
    The charms of her lovely and beautiful face,
    When to his surprisement she vanished away;
    He went to the captain without more delay,

13. "There is a ghost appeared in the dead of the night,
    And all our brave sailors are terribly afright;
    Our men has done murder and if this be true,
    Our ship's in great danger if to sea she will go."

14. William declared and avowed that nothing he knew,
    But straight from the captain he offered to go;
    That night as William in his cabin did lie,
    The voice of his true love was heard for to cry.

15. "Rise up prodigious Willie so soon you shall hear
    The voice of your true love that loved you so dear";
    "O yonder stands Mary and where shall I run?
    Pray somebody save me or I'll be undone."

16. She shrieked and she vanished; she screamed and she cried;
    The flashes of lightning flew from her eyes;
    She put all the ship crew in a terrible fright,
    And raving distracted William died that night.

17. In groves of Hamilton where valleys are deep,
    Her body was found where so many do sleep;
    She in her arms held a baby so fair,
    And in Gospel churchyard, they buried her there. (70-1A)

The Boston Burglar

1. I was born in Boston,
   A city you all know well,
   Brought up by honest parents;
   The truth to you I'll tell,
   Brought up by honest parents,
   Raised most tenderly,
   Till I became a sporting lad
   At the age of twenty-three.

2. Then my character was taken;
   I was sent to jail.
   My friends, they found quite in vain
   For to get me out on bail;
   The jury found me guilty,

The clerk, he wrote it down,
The judge, he passed the sentence;
I was sent to Charlesontown,

3. To see my dear aged father
Come pleading at the bar;
Likewise my ancient mother
Come tearing down her hair,
Come tearing down her gray old locks,
While the tears began to run,
Saying, "Son, oh son, what have you done,
That you're sent to Charlesontown?"

4. I was put on board an eastern train,
On a cold December day,
And every station I passed by,
I heard the people say,
"There goes that Boston burglar;
In iron chains he'll be bound,
For some bad deed or other,
He is sent to Charlesontown."

5. I have a girl in Boston,
A girl that I love well;
If ever I gain my liberty,
Along with her I'll dwell;
If ever I gain my liberty,
Bad company I'll shun;
Likewise like walking gambler,
And also drinking rum.

6. All you having your liberty,
Pray keep it if you can,
And don't go 'round the streets at night,
And break the laws of man;
For if you do you'll surely rue,
And find yourselves like me,
While serving out my twenty-one years,
In the penitentiary. (H)

Lucky Old Town O

1. The old fox hopped out one moonshiny night;
He hopped on his left foot just about right;
"What shall I have for my supper tonight?

Before I lie myself down O,
Down O, down O,
Before I lie myself down O."

2. He marched right up to the old farmer's stile;
   The gray goose, she began to whimper and to smile;
   "Gray goose, gray goose, stay a little while,
   And I'll take you to my lucky old town O,
   Town O, town O,
   And I'll take you to my lucky old town O."

3. He caught the gray goose by the back of the neck;
   Her wings went flip, flop, flip, flop, flip,
   And her feet hung dingle, dingle, down O,
   Down O, down O,
   And her feet hung dingle, dingle, dingle, down O.

4. The old woman jumped up out of her bed;
   Out a broken windowpane she poked her head;
   "Old man, old man, don't you know,
   The fox's got the gray goose and taken her to his lucky
        old town O,
   Town O, town O,
   And taken her to his lucky old town O."

5. When the old fox he came to his den,
   Out ran some young ones, eight or nine or ten;
   "Daddy dear, Daddy dear, how came you with this?"
   "I came by my lucky old town O,
   Town O, town O,
   I came by my lucky old town O." (70-1A)

Proverbs and Proverbial Speech. In addition to tales and songs, a great number of shorter forms of folklore exist in Maryland, and often these shorter items have a tendency to persevere in tradition with little or no change simply because, being short, they are easily remembered. Also, these short items fall easily into everyday speech patterns and thus are kept fresh in the minds of the people who use them and hear them. A proverb, for instance, would be much more likely to serve an illustrative point in a conversation ("A penny saved is a penny earned"; "Absence makes the heart grow fonder.") than would a long explanatory tale or fable or moralistic folksong. We know for a fact that the proverb has been, and still is, used in both urban and rural homes as an indirect form of education as well as a modified kind of admonishment. Some proverbs, as can be seen, state their wisdom in the straight apothegm while others observe a truth metaphorically. To note a few very common ones from Maryland:

> If you run with wolves, you've got to howl.[8]
>
> A barking dog never bites.
>
> Idle hands are the devil's workshop.
>
> A word to the wise is sufficient.
>
> Birds of a feather stick together.
>
> The empty wagon rattles loudest.
>
> Beauty is as beauty does.
>
> A new broom sweeps clean.
>
> An ounce of prevention is worth a pound of cure.
>
> Even a dumb squirrel will find an acorn once in a while.
>
> Every tub has to sit on its own bottom.
>
> Sow your wild oats on Saturday night; then go to church on Sunday and pray for crop failure.
>
> Home is where the heart is.
>
> Promises, like pie crusts, are easily broken.
>
> Where there's smoke, there's fire.
>
> Who knows most, says least.
>
> A constant guest is never welcome.
>
> When an ass goes a-traveling, he never comes back a horse.
>
> Little pitchers have big ears.
>
> You can't teach an old dog new tricks.
>
> Willful waste makes woeful want.
>
> Absence makes the heart grow fonder (go wander).
>
> Short accounts make long friends.
>
> In the realm of the blind, the one-eyed are kings.
>
> Life is short and full of blisters.
>
> There are more flies to be caught with honey than with vinegar.

What's good for the goose is good for the gander.

to buy a pig in a poke

to cut your nose off to spite your face

to put your foot in your mouth

not to know your ass from a hole in the ground

to know which side your bread is buttered on

to have champagne tastes with a beer pocketbook

to have a face that would stop a clock

in one ear and out the other

Don't put the cart before the horse.

Show me the company you keep and I'll tell you what you
    are.

Sprinkled throughout all of folk speech is another common type of proverb called the proverbial comparison. It is highly flexible and appears in innumerable forms, most of which are traditional:

as easy as pie

skinny as a beanpole

dark as the inside of a cow

as ugly as a mud fence

as easy as falling off a log

tighter than the wallpaper on the wall

as big as a house

so thin he has to drink muddy water to cast a shadow

pretty as a steamboat

dark as pitch

so tough he used to go out every morning before breakfast
    with a wildcat under each arm looking for chestnut burrs
    to wipe his hind end with

hungry as a bear

crazy as a loon

drunk as a skunk

so foolish he can't pour piss out of a boot with the directions on the heel

as busy as a bee in a tar bucket

as happy as a clam at high tide

so ugly she has to sneak up on a glass to get a drink of water

as dumb as an oyster

as polite as a dog pissing on a briar

black as sin

snug as a bug in a rug

bright as a button

as tight as beeswax

He has as much use for that as a hog does for a ruffled shirt.

busier than a one-armed paper hanger

cold as a well-digger's ass

as crazy as Tom Curtz's dog

grinning like a mule eating briars

slick as snot and not half so greasy

crooked as a dog's hind leg

He's got eyes like two holes in a blanket.

That's enough to piss off the Good Humor man.

Another form of proverbial expression is the Wellerism, and though it was much more common a century or more ago, the traditional phrases still linger in Maryland. The form differs slightly from the usual proverb in that we learn from the context exactly who said it and when.

"Every little bit helps," said the wren as she spit in the sea.
"I see," said the blind man to his deaf daughter.
"Everybody to his own liking," said the woman as she kissed the cow.
"That's punishing her with good words," said the preacher as he threw the Bible at his wife.

"It all comes back to me now," said the captain as he spit into the wind.

As Kinsey said, "You're O.K. in my book."

"It won't be long now," said the cat as she backed her tail into the lawnmower.

Riddles and Tongue Twisters. Riddling as an art is one of the oldest forms of oral tradition. One thinks of Samson's riddle in the Bible (*Judges*, xiv, 14):

Out of the eater came forth meat,
And out of the strong came forth sweetness.
—Honeycomb in a lion's carcass.

Not all riddles are as complex as Samson's, however, for most of them contain enough information so that the listener can solve them. There is ample evidence to make us believe that several generations ago in certain communities in Maryland the riddle served as a vital means of adult entertainment, both at home and at local gathering places. Traditional riddles were employed to sharpen the wits of children and grownups alike, and in more religiously inclined areas question-and-answer sessions on esoteric matters in the Bible frequently gave rise to humorous situations, as this story from Smith Island illustrates:

To give you some prelude to what they did on the island, they'd get around this store there, and they would look at the Bible and they would get things to stump each other with, you know. So this guy came in; Mitch Evans, but they called him Will Torg. So he came into the store one time and said, 'I guess I got one that will stump you. Does anyone know how long King Solomon's been dead?'

Well, nobody knew, and just about this time this character walked in there. It was Harry Low, and somebody said, 'Captain Mitch, ask Harry.'

And Captain Mitchell stood up and said, 'Harry, do you know?'

'Know what, Captain Mitchell?'

'Do you know how long King Solomon's been dead?'

Harry said, 'Well, hell, man, I didn't even know he'd been sick.' (ES 70-1)

But for the most part the riddling contests along with folksinging contests have given way to other things. Even the children who never seem to tire of mental gymnastics have virtually abandoned the traditional riddle and replaced it with the *non sequitur* amusement of the sham riddle. For example: "Why do elephants drink?" Answer: "To forget." "What is green, weighs 2000 pounds, and lives in the ocean?" Answer: "Moby Pickle." Still, if one speaks to the right person in the right community, he can invariably uncover some of the older forms of riddle, if not actively passed along, certainly remembered. A selective sampling from throughout the state provides a sense of the riddling tradition.

> Old Mother Twitchett had but one eye,
> And a long thread which she let fly;
> And every time she went over a gap,
> She left a little bit of her tail caught in a trap.
> (A needle and thread)

> In marble walls as white as milk,
> Lined with a skin as soft as silk;
> Within a fountain crystal clear,
> A golden apple doth appear.
> No doors there are to this stronghold,
> Yet thieves break in and steal the gold.
> (Egg)

> Thirty white horses upon a white hill,
> Now they tramp, now they champ, now they stand still.
> (Teeth)

> Little Nancy Etticoat,
> In a white petticoat, and a red nose;
> The longer she stands,
> The shorter she grows.
> (Candle)

> Out in the meadow is a little red bull,
> He eats and eats, but never gets full.
> (A threshing machine)

> As round as a coin,
> Busy as a bee;
> The prettiest little thing
> You ever did see.
> (Watch)

> What shoemaker makes shoes without leather,
> With all four elements put together?
> Fire, water, earth, and air;
> Every customer has two pair.
> (Horseshoer)

A riddle, riddle, I suppose,
A thousand eyes, yet never a nose.
(Thimble)

Two lookers, two crookers,
Four hang-downs, one switch-about.
What is it?
(A cow)

Patch upon patch and hole in the middle,
Tell me this riddle and I'll give you a gold fiddle.
(Chimney)

As I was going across London Bridge, I met old Daddy
   Gray.
I ate his meat and drank his blood,
And threw his bones away.
Now just who is Daddy Gray?
(An oyster)

As I was going across London Bridge,
I met my sister Ann.
I cut her throat and sucked her blood,
And let her body stand.
(Bottle of whiskey)

Two little brothers,
Both the same burden bear;
The colder the weather,
The hotter the air.
(Andirons)

Over, over, in between,
Heart-shaped tents of shining green;
I spread gay skirts to greet the sun,
Then fold them close, my work is done.
(Morning Glory)

Black without, red within,
Pick up your foot and stick it in.
(Boot)

I have legs but cannot walk;
A leaf, but I'm no tree;
I may be square or round or long—
Sometimes you sit by me.
(Table)

I have eyes, but cannot see,
A skin but not a face.

When farmers dig up ground for me,
They find my hiding place.
(Irish potato)

What goes all over the house during the day
And sits in the corner at night?
(Broom)

What won't go up the chimney up,
But will go up the chimney down,
And won't go down the chimney up,
But will go down the chimney down?
(Umbrella)

What goes up- and downstairs on its head?
(Shoe nail)

If a dog's front legs are traveling thirty miles per hour,
What are his hind legs doing?
(Hauling tail)

What goes up and never comes down?
(Your age)

House full, yard full, and can't catch a cup full.
(Smoke)

We have tongues, but never talk,
Some eyes, but never see.
You take us with you when you walk;
Now what can such things be?
(Shoes)

What is it that a poor man puts on the ground that a rich
    man puts in his pocket?
(Snot)

What do you cut off at both ends to make longer?
(A ditch)

Twelve pears hanging high,
Twelve men came riding by,
Each man took a pear,
And left eleven hanging there.
How could this be?
(Man's name was Each)

Belly to belly, arm around the back,
Big lump of fat meat to fill up the crack.
(Mother nursing her child)

What's long, slim and slender, tickles where it's tender and
    hurts where the thing goes?
(Whip)

Under my apron there's a little round hole,
If you please to believe it's as black as coal.
You can pull it, you can stretch it,
You can do it no harm.
You can put a thing in it as long as your arm.
What is it?
(Woman knitting a black stocking with her needles and
    yarn)

It's thin, long, stiff, and slender,
You stick it in and wiggle it about,
And then the juice comes running out.
What is it?
(Shucking an oyster)

I went to the field and got it.
I took it home in my hand because I couldn't find it.
The more I looked for it, the more it hurt.
And when I found it I threw it away.
(Thorn)

What's the best way to make a coat last?
(Make the vest first)

Why is a room of married people like an empty room?
(Not a single person in it)

Like the riddle, the tongue twister entertains both child and adult.
Frequently used by adults, these difficult word arrangements allow
the speaker to utter an obscenity simply because his tongue is
tangled, and thus, a taboo is broken within the framework of the oral
game making it both acceptable and amusing. Some of the tongue
twisters known in Maryland include:

She sells sea shells; shall he sell sea shells?

Shave a cedar shingle thin.

Frank threw Fred three free throws.

Tillie's twin sweater set.

Fred threads red thread.

A fly and a flea were caught in a flue one day.
Said the flea, "Let's fly," said the fly, "Let's flee."
So they flew through the flaw in the flue.

He sawed six long, slim, slender, slick saplings.

Sweet Sally Sanders said she saw seven segregated seagulls
sailing swiftly southwest, Saturday.

I'm a fig plucker, I pluck figs. I'm the best darn fig plucker
that ever plucked a fig.

A big black buffalo blew bubbles.

An old scold sold a cold coal shovel.

She sits in her slip and sips Schlitz.

Two toads totally tired tried to trot to Tadbury.

rubber baby buggy bumpers

Theophilus Thistle, the cross-eyed thistle sifter.

Tongue twisters frequently fuse with riddles as in this esoteric
description of someone watching a bear tear up his fence:

As I went up to hazel-dazel,
I looked out the razzle dazzle;
I saw old mother middlecum-maddlecum
Tearing up my striddlecum-straddlecum.
If I'd had my diddlecum-daddlecum,
I'd have shot old mother middlecum-maddlecum.

Or they become part of a long jingle or short song.

Sammy was a sailor, a sailor brave and bold;
He shipped aboard a whaler and tumbled overboard.
He shouted, "Someone save me,"
And someone said, "Go hang."
The sharks were swimming madly as the sailors sang:

"Swim Sam, swim Sam, swim Sam,
Show them you're some swimmer;
Swim like Snow White's swans swim,
You know, like Snow White's swans swim.
Six white shimmering sharks are out to get your limbs,
So a swim well swum is a well swum swim,
So swim, Sam, swim Sam, swim Sam." (69-83)

Children's Games and Traditions. Students of children's games have found them one of the most intriguing aspects of folklore when it comes to examining just how traditions are passed along. Played in truly unconscious fashion by the children, these games often reach back over a thousand years and reveal an enamel which has held them together through time. A glance at Lady Gomme's *Traditional Games of England, Scotland, and Ireland,* published at the end of the nineteenth century, makes it evident that the games played and the rhymes uttered by children 75 years ago are still current on the sidewalks of Bethesda and the playgrounds of Baltimore. And the reason for this amazing persistence of tradition lies in the very nature of the children themselves. Innately intolerant at a young age, they teach newcomers their games in a very strict way, ostracizing them when they cannot learn the jingle correctly or make the right and necessary moves. Often there is a more efficient learning process taking place on the concrete of the playground than in the theoretically more conducive atmosphere of the classroom.

Children's games appear in incredible variety. They include, to mention a few types: chasing games, guessing games, forfeit games, ball games, hiding games, and jumping and hopping games. Often the games are accompanied by some kind of oral utterance, as in the rhymes and jingles that provide a rhythmic aid to jumping rope. Though children's games tend to stay very much the same over a period of time, there are obvious alterations that will occur, as in this updated game of "T.V. Tag" reported in Salisbury.

> One person is IT. The others run and if they squat down and say the name of a T.V. show, they're safe. If you get caught before you get out the name of a T.V. program, then you have to be IT. (ES 69-8)

More elaborate is this widely known game, called in this version (also from Salisbury) "Donna Died":

> There is a circle game, with one girl in the middle. She stands and goes through motions or answers the questions that the girls in the outside circle ask. They chant: 'Donna died. How did she die?' The girl in the center shows this answer by going through some action. She acts out the answer. The girls in the outer ring ask: 'Where did she live?' The girl answers: 'Tennessee.'
> The group says: 'Wear their dresses up above their knees,' and the girls all pull their dresses up above the knee.

 The girl in the middle circles and points to another in the outer ring. Then everybody chants this rhyme:

She never went to college,
She never went to school;
We all found out
She's an educated fool.

Then the girl who was pointed at goes into the middle and the whole thing starts all over again. (ES 69-8)

Sampling other children's games in Maryland, one is struck by the similarity of the games as played in different places throughout the state. In fact, the thing that appears to alter most in the game is the name, and the naming is imaginative indeed. To wit: "Buttons on the Steps," "Beast, Bird, or Fish," "I'm Going to Jerusalem," "Fox in the Morning," "Ghost in the Graveyard," "Duck, Duck, Goose," "Candy Kisses Game," "My Father Owns a Grocery Store." A representative selection of traditional games collected in Maryland includes:

Red Light, Green Light

One child is chosen to be the leader who calls, 'Red light.' He stands some distance from the other children while they remain at the starting line. While he is counting to ten with his back to the other children they run towards him to reach him and tag him. However, when he calls, 'Red light,' all the children must stop and not move. If he catches anyone moving they are out of the game. If anyone gets to tag him before he finishes counting and before he says, 'Red light,' that child is the leader for the next game. (69-156)

Giant Steps

One person is chosen to be 'mother' and stands a few feet in front of the rest of the players behind a line. The 'mother' tells each person, in turn, a certain kind and number of steps to take and before doing this, the player must say, 'Mother, may I?' Failure to do this means the player must go back to the line and start over again. The first person to reach 'mother' is the new leader. Some of the steps that 'mother' would use were the following: scissors steps, umbrella steps, giant steps, baby steps and elephant steps. The 'mother' could make up new steps and name them herself, so long as she demonstrated them. (H)

Button, Button, Who's Got the Button?

A button or some other small object was used to play this game. The players either stood or were seated in a line and one person had the button. With the button in his hand, the leader gave each person a chance to guess which hand it was in. If he missed he was eliminated from the game. The last person in the game was the next leader.

I played this game while attending the Dickerson Elementary School in Dickerson, Maryland. The children who played it ranged from six to twelve years of age. (H)

Huckle Buckle Beanstalk

An object is shown to all the children. Then three children are picked to leave the room. One child takes the object and hides it. It must be in sight but must also be hard to find. The three children return to the room and look for the object. The first child to spot it says, 'Huckle buckle beanstalk,' and goes and sits down. The other children also try to find it and when they do, they say the same thing. The child who sees the object first gets to be the one to hide it the next time. (69-156)

Fox and Geese

Outdoors draw a large wheel with spokes. Choose one person to be the fox. The rest of the kids are the geese. At the word 'Go,' the fox chases the geese through the spokes and the rim of the wheel without touching the spaces in-between or the space outside the wheel. The goose who is caught then becomes the fox and the game begins again. (68-23)

Swinging Statues

One kid was the swinger. He swung the other kids around and let go of them and they were supposed to freeze in a certain position and not move. If they moved they were disqualified. The swinger chose the best looking position and picked one, and that kid got to be the swinger the next time. (68-23)

Upset the Fruit Basket

The players sit around in a circle. Each player is given a name that is the name of a fruit. These names are divided into pairs; that is, two people to the same fruit. An extra person is placed in the center of the circle. She calls a fruit and the two people who are that fruit try and exchange seats. Meanwhile, the girl in the middle also tries to get one of the seats. The person left over then becomes the leader. If the person in the middle does get the seat away, she assumes the name of that fruit. The person in the center may call 'Upset the fruit basket,' and then everyone changes seats and again the person left over is the leader. My friends used to play this in elementary school in Frederick, Maryland. (H)

Ruth and Jacob

This game is a variation of 'Blind Man's Bluff.' The person chosen to be IT is blindfolded. The other players walk around within a set boundary. The blindfolded person calls 'Ruth' and the other must answer, 'Jacob.' The game continues in this manner until someone is caught. When someone is caught, the person IT must identify whoever he has caught. Then the person caught becomes IT. I used to play this game in Beltsville, Maryland, when I was about ten years old. (H)

Punch a 'Nella

This game has a rhyme to it:

Look who's here,
Punch a 'nella funny fella,
Look who's here
Punch a 'nella funny you.

What can you do,
Punch a 'nella funny fella?
What can you do,
Punch a 'nella funny you?

We can do it too,
Punch a 'nella funny fella
We can do it too
Punch a 'nella funny you.

Who do you choose
Punch a 'nella funny fella?
Who do you choose
Punch a 'nella funny you?

One player is Punch and the others form a circle around him. The first verse of the rhyme has no actions. During the second verse Punch does some simple actions and the others join in the third verse. On the fourth verse Punch closes his eyes and turns in a circle while the others turn in the opposite direction. At the end of the fourth verse, everyone stops and the person at whom Punch is pointing is the next Punch. This game is usually played by children about six years old. (H)

Rhymes appear in other types of children's play lore as, for instance, in the counting-out rhymes to find out who will be IT in a game, or who will be the rope turner for jump-rope. "I lit a match and put it O-U-T" would choose the person that the "T" fell on and the same thing would hold for the last word of these counting-out rhymes.

1-2-3-4,
Mary at the cottage door.
5-6-7-8,
Eating cherries off a plate.
O-U-T spells out.

Fish, fish
In the dish,
How many fishes do you wish?

Out goes the rat,
Out goes the cat,
Out goes the lady with the see-saw hat.
O-U-T spells out.
So you go out. (H)

Though rhyming occurs frequently in children's games the world over, perhaps no rhymes or chants spring to their lips more imaginatively than those uttered when they jump rope. The profusion of names, places, characters, objects and situations which crop up again and again, in these jingles, as the rope is turned and the jumper steps in to perform, again reveals the breadth of childhood fancy. Some samples from a collection of jump-rope rhymes from Kensington, Maryland, suggest the variety.

Winstons taste good, like a cigarette should,
Winstons taste good, like a oompa oompa,

Want a piece of meat?
Pie too sweet, want a piece of meat,
Meat too tough, want to ride a bus,
Bus too full, want to ride a bull,
Bull too black, want to ride a Cadillac.
Cadillac too new, want to ride a gnu.
Gnu too big, want to pick some figs.
(Jumper keeps going until he misses or fails to make up
   a rhyme.)

Teddybear, teddybear, touch the ground,
Teddybear, teddybear, turn around,
Teddybear, teddybear, jump up and down,
Teddybear, teddybear, get out of town.

Not last night but the night before,
Twenty-four robbers knocking at my door.
As I awoke I found this note,
And this is what it said to me:
'Spanish dancer, give a high kick,
Spanish dancer, turn around,
Spanish dancer, touch the ground,
Spanish dancer, get out of town.'

I'm a little Dutch girl, dressed in blue,
These are the actions that I can do:
Salute to the captain,
Curtsy to the queen,
Touch the bottom of the submarine.
If you touch it ten more times,
You may get your turn again.

Down in the valley where the green grass grows,
There sat Julie as sweet as a rose.
She sang, she sang, she sang so sweet,
Along came Bill and kissed her on the cheek.
How many kisses did she receive?
(Jumper jumps until she misses.) (70-56)

From Easton comes a version of "Johnny Over the Ocean," a
widely known rhyme which interestingly enough dates back to a
Scottish Jacobite song of 1748 that dealt with Bonnie Prince Charlie.

Johnny over the ocean,
Johnny over the sea,
Johnny broke the milk bottle—
Blamed it on me.

I told brother,
Brother told sister,
Sister told mother,
Mother told father.

Father gave Johnny
Some RED HOT PEPPER! (68-41)

From the streets of Baltimore come several well-known rhymes:

I wish I had a nickel,
I wish I had a dime,
I wish I had a boyfriend,
To love me all the time.

My mother gave me a nickel,
My father gave me a dime,
My sister gave me a boyfriend,
To kiss me all the time.

My mother took my nickel,
My father took my dime,
My sister took my boyfriend,
And gave me Frankenstein.

He made me wash the dishes,
He made me wash the floor,
He made me so disgusted,
I kicked him out the door.

• • • •

Miss Lucy had a baby,
She called him Tiny Tim;
She put him in the bathtub,
To see if he could swim.

He drank up all the water,
He ate up all the soap;
He tried to eat the bathtub,
But it wouldn't go down his throat.

Miss Lucy called the doctor,
Miss Lucy called the nurse,
Miss Lucy called a lady,
With an alligator purse.

Out came the water,
Out came the soap,
Out came the bathtub,
That wouldn't go down his throat.

• • • •

Fudge, fudge, call the judge,
Mama's got a newborn baby.
It's not a boy; it's not a girl,
It's just a newborn baby.

Wrap him up in tissue paper,
Send him down the elevator.
First floor—miss
Second floor—miss
Third floor—miss.

Send for the doctor,
Send for the nurse,
Send for the lady,
With the alligator purse.

'Mumps,' said the doctor,
'Measles,' said the nurse.
'Dead,' said the lady
With the alligator purse.

• • • •

Cinderella,
Dressed in yellow,
Went downtown
To see her fellow.

She made a mistake
And kissed a snake.
How many doctors did it take?
One, two, three, four . . . . (70-49)

Black children in Baltimore provide more variations:

> When the sun shines through the leaves of the apple tree,
> When the sun makes shadows on the leaves of the apple tree,
> Then I pass, on the grass,
> From my leaf to another,
> From one leaf to its brother.
> Tip-toe, here I go; tip-toe, here I go.
> (Jump till you miss.)

> Charlie Chaplin went to France
> To teach the girls the hula dance;
> A heel, a toe, around we go.
> Salute to the captain,
> Bow to the queen,
> Touch the bottom of the submarine.

> Apple on a stick,
> Make me sick,
> Make my heart go forty-six.
> Not because it's dirty,
> Not because it's clean,
> Not because the kissy boy behind the magazine.

> George Washington never told a lie,
> He went 'round and stole a cherry pie.
> How many cherries was in that pie?
> One, two, three, ... (69-42)

If jump-rope rhymes furnish proof of children's ability to keep jingles alive in oral tradition, so do their autograph books provide evidence that this same group has been active in the persistence of another verse form. One need only compare autograph books from the turn of the century with those of last year to see that the rhymes themselves, though occasionally updated, have changed very little. It might be speculated that autograph verse, like the graffiti found on subway and bathroom walls, allows an individual to pen his thought and his name to something that will last longer than he. In the words of a well-known graffito, "Rose was here,/ And now she's gone,/ But left her name/ To carry on." From a Maryland autograph book a similar sentiment is struck:

> O remember me by the looks I make,
> O remember me by your gum I take,
> O remember me by the way I walk,
> O remember me by the way I talk,
> O remember me by my name,
> For I write it now
> In your book of fame. (69-106)

Whatever the underlying reason for inscribing one's name in a book of autograph verse, the writer inevitably signs it under traditional rhymes such as these written by Marylanders:

When you get old
And think you're sweet,
Take off your shoes
And smell your feet.

2 sweet
2 be
4 gotten.

I take me pen,
I take me ink;
Me scratch me head,
And then me think.
Me think, me think,
Me think in vain;
Me think me better
Sign me name.

Roses are red,
Violets are blue;
A face like yours
Belongs in the zoo.

Boys are bad,
Beds are worse,
Sleep alone,
Safety first.

ICURAQT

INVU

I know a girl in the city,
I know a girl in the town;
I'm the girl who spoiled your book
By writing upside down.

First comes love,
Then comes marriage;
Then comes Irma
With a baby carriage. (69-106)

I wish you luck,
I wish you joy,
I wish you first a baby boy,
And when his hair begins to curl,
I wish you then a baby girl.
And when you start to use pins,
I wish you then a pair of twins.

Love many, trust few—
Always paddle your own canoe.

While sliding down the banister of life,
Think of me as a splinter in your career.

Roses are red
Violets are black;
You'd look better
With a knife in your back.

When you get married
And buy a Ford,
Save me room
On the running board.

Yours till America gets Hungary and eats Turkey. (H)

Folk Belief. One noted scholar has claimed that folk belief is the common denominator of folklore.[9] What he has in mind, it seems, is that superstition or folk belief appears in practically every kind of orally transmitted lore. We find belief appearing in song, in tale, in proverb, riddle, and children's games. The spectrum of folk belief covers the entire life cycle, starting with conception, pregnancy, and birth and moving through death, burial, and return from the dead. As Alan Dundes has pointed out, most superstitions contain either a sign and result or a cause and result.[10] Most token beliefs fall into this category. To wit: "If you see a falling star (sign), a loved one will die (result)." "If a picture falls off the wall (sign), someone is going to die (result)." Or with cause and result: "To hang a tea towel on the doorknob (cause), is a sure sign of death (result)." "When two look in the mirror at the same time (cause), the younger will die (result)." Magic enters folk belief quite noticeably when one attempts to convert the simple cause and result omen into good luck. For example: "If you spill salt (cause), you will get a beating (result), unless you throw some of it over your shoulder (conversion)." With the bad luck induced by a black cat crossing one's path, several conversions are possible: "go back, sit down, and cross your legs six times before going on"; "turn around three times to break the spell"; "spit in a hat."

In collecting beliefs, the folklorist attempts to discern exactly what role they play in the lives of informants. Are they believed or only remembered? A tape recording of a conversation with an Eastern Shore waterman reveals what might be a typical reaction of an informant to a belief familiar to him:

> Collector: Captain, have you ever heard about something they call 'buying the wind' around here?
> Informant: Yes, I've heard people say if you throw a penny overboard there'd come a breeze. I don't know if it really works.
> Collector: Have you ever tried it?
> Informant: Yeah, I done it once over here in Pocomoke Sound and there come a nice little breeze, but that didn't have nothing to do with that. (ES 70-1)

One attempting to gather and study Maryland's rich bounty of folk beliefs will find that despite the average person's suspicion that a belief is peculiar to one region, in most cases Maryland superstitions are known throughout the country and, in certain instances, throughout the world. The scope of belief pattern is only hinted at in this random sampling from throughout the state.

Love, Courtship and Marriage.

The number of white spots on your fingernails indicates the number of boyfriends you have.

If you give a knife to your sweetheart, it will cut the love in two.

If you burn a match and it breaks, your love is not true, but if the match burns to the end, your love is true and coming to you from the direction the match points.

Put a snail in a tray of soft sand and he will spell out the initials of your husband-to-be.

Put a wishbone over the doorway and the first man to come through under it will be the man you will marry.

From LaVale, Maryland: When I was a young girl a popular thing with the young girls was the 'dumb supper.' This took place at midnight and was served entirely backwards. At midnight your future husband was supposed to appear at the head of the table. One night my sister and I decided to attend one of these suppers. We had prepared everything and just as the clock struck twelve, the wind began to howl and all the cows ran from the hills and gathered around the house and then there was a shattering noise like chains hitting the doorsteps and my sister and I ran frightened to bed and never stayed to see our future husbands appear.

From the Eastern Shore: Boil an egg and fill it with pepper. Set a place on the table and put it there. Open the door and turn the lights down low and at midnight the wind will blow and the man who comes in and eats the egg will be your husband.

Reach for the doorknob at the wrong side of the door and you won't get married that year.

If you wet the front of your dress while washing the dishes, you'll marry a drunkard.

If you eat the last piece of food on your plate, you'll be an old maid.

A fifty-cent piece in a bride's shoe insures prosperity in the marriage.

If your eyebrows grow together when you're a teenager, you've already met the man you'll marry.

If you wear someone else's wedding or engagement ring, you'll never marry.

If you dream of death, a wedding will take place in the family.

Change the name and not the letter,
Is to change for worse and not for better.

Birth, Infancy, and Childhood.

If a new baby is put on the bed of a married woman who is trying to conceive, she will become pregnant.

If you dream of fresh fish, someone in the house is pregnant.

If your apron comes untied, you'll soon have something to fill it out with.

If a pregnant woman is shaped round, the baby will be a boy; if she looks pointed, it will be a girl.

If a pregnant woman has a craving for some kind of food and doesn't get it, her baby will be marked with that food.

A pregnant woman should place a knife under the bed as that is good for cutting the pains.

If a pregnant woman is frightened, her baby will wear the birthmark of the thing that frightened her.

If you don't bite a baby's fingernails off when they get long, he'll steal when he gets older.

Don't let a baby see himself in the mirror or he will cut his teeth hard.

Put a bottle, a Bible and a piece of money in front of a baby. If he touches the Bible first, he will become a preacher; if he touches the money first, he will become a banker; if he touches the bottle first, he will become a drunkard.

If you rock an empty baby cart, you'll give the baby colic.

When an infant loses the navel cord, it must be burned; if you throw it away, the child will wet his bed as he grows older.

The seventh child, born on the seventh day, can see visions.

A baby born with a veil of afterbirth over its face will grow up to be a prophet.

If you tickle a baby's feet, it will cause him to stammer.

Home Pursuits.

If you put your clothing on inside out, it's bad luck to change it.

If the hem of your dress turns up, spit on it and you'll receive a new one.

If your nose itches, a stranger is coming.

If you drop a knife, a man is coming; if you drop a fork, a woman is coming.

For good luck, always stir the cake batter in the same direction.

A visitor must always go out the same entrance he came in.

When you leave home, it's bad luck to go back for something you forgot.

Never let a woman be the first one in your house on New Year's Day, or you'll have bad luck all year long.

If your ears burn, someone is talking about you.

It's bad luck to give an empty pocketbook.

It's bad luck for two people to look in the mirror at the same time.

See a pin, pick it up,
All the day you'll have good luck.
See a pin, let it lay,
Bad luck will come all the day.

It's bad luck to sew on Sunday; if you do, you'll have to pull every stitch out with your nose after you die.

When someone is sewing a button onto a piece of cloth while you are wearing it, chew on a piece of thread or place the tip end of the collar of your dress in your mouth and chew on it to keep from sewing up your sense.

Never iron your husband's shirt tails or else he will be cross.

Make soap on the increase of the moon; it will thicken better.

If you sing before breakfast, you'll cry before dark.

It's bad luck to put a loaf of bread upside down.

If you sweep the floor after six p.m., don't pick up the dirt. Leave it until morning or you'll have bad luck.

If a broom hits you while someone's sweeping, it's a sign you'll go to jail.

Death Beliefs.

If a dog howls, it's a sign of death.

If a rooster crows on the back doorstep once, company is coming; if he crows three times, death will come to someone in the house.

A black bird on the window sill means death.

If a bird flies into the house, it's a sign of death.

To hang a tea towel on the doorknob is a sure sign there's going to be a death in the family.

Dropping food from your mouth while you're eating is a sign of death.

If you rock an empty rocking chair, someone in the house will die.

If you hear a screech owl, there will be a death in the family; but if you tie a knot in the corner of your bedsheet, the death will be averted.

If you have a mole on the heel of your left foot, you will die young.

If you accidentally skip a row while planting seed, there will be a death in the family before the crop is harvested.

If a tree or shrub blooms out of season, it's a sign of death in the family.

If there's a death in your family and you don't rap on each beehive, all the bees will leave.

Don't count the cars in a funeral procession or someone else will die.

A green Christmas means a fat graveyard in the spring.

Animals, Animal Husbandry, and Planting.

If you have varmints in your house, catch seven and pin them over your back door. Whoever goes out the back door first takes all the varmints with him and you are rid of them for good.

If pigs' tails turn to the right, it's safe for breeding; if they turn to the left, it's not.

To be sure eggs will hatch, put nails under the pine shats in the nest.

A cat that rests on a baby will steal its breath away.

Cut some hair out of a dog's tail and put it under the house, and he will stay home.

About magpies: See one, that's for sorrow,
　　　　　　　See two, that's for mirth,
　　　　　　　See three, that's a wedding,
　　　　　　　See four, that's a birth,
　　　　　　　See five, that's for silver,
　　　　　　　See six, that's for gold,
　　　　　　　See seven, that's for a secret, never
　　　　　　　　to be told.

In order to break the bad luck of a cat crossing in front of you, spit in your hat. My uncle carried an old hat in his car just for that purpose, and I've seen him use it more than once.

If you kill a snake and hang it over the fence, it will rain.

When you cut down a bee tree, always say 'eema, eema' and they can't sting you.

If a snapping turtle bites you, it will hang on 'til the sun goes down.

Plant all underground crops on the dark of the moon for a better yield.

Never plant beans when the wind is from the northeast; they will create too much wind after being eaten.

When the whippoorwill hollers in the spring, it's time to plant corn.

If you plant lima beans by the light of a lantern, the crop will be plentiful.

Weather Beliefs.

The weather the last Friday of each month determines the weather for the month to come.

Rain before seven, clear by eleven.

Evening red and morning gray,
Sends the traveler on his way.
Evening gray and morning red,
Sends down rain upon his head.

A rooster that crows when he goes to bed
Will get up next morning with a wet head.

A sunshiny shower
Won't last an hour.

Red sky at night, sailor's delight;
Red sky in the morning, sailors take warning.

When crows flock together, it's a sign of bad weather.

If a cat passes its paw over its ear, it's a sign of rain.

A high hornet's nest is a sign of deep snow coming.

When you see raindrops hanging on the clothline [sic], you know it will rain again tomorrow.

It will be a long winter if bands on caterpillars are narrow, leaves are slow to fall, squirrels grow unusually bushy tails, skin of the belly of a catfish is unusually thick, the breastbone of a chicken is long and black.

Onion skin thick and tough,
Coming winter will be rough.
Onion skin very thin,
Mild winter coming in.

When the horns of the moon point down, it will rain.

It will snow if turkeys sit in the trees and refuse to come down, cats sit with their back to the fire, dry leaves rattle in the trees, burning wood drops in the fire, air becomes still and silent.

If the smoke of the chimney floats towards the ground, this is a sign of rain.

The number of stars in the circle around the moon tell the number of days before a storm will come.

If the fog lifts,
The rain will fall;
If the fog descends,
No rain at all.

Folk Medicine. A large segment of folk belief hinges on the traditional practices carried out in the area of folk medicine. Belief in the efficacy of folk healers, or "pow-wows" as they are known in some parts of Maryland, has fostered an active trade in folk medicine over the years. One Eastern Shore informant recalled:

Now there was this girl and she was burned real bad—third-degree burns and the flesh just running right off her and so they said, 'You'd better go and see Miss Emmy.' So they took her down and she didn't use any ointment or anything. Just rubbed her hands along those burns and when that girl healed, there wasn't one scar on her anywhere. (ES 70-1)

In another part of the state, healers "blew the fire out," as a woman from Brunswick, Maryland, explained:

Mrs. Shelton lives up the street from grandmother, and grandmother took me up there to ask her about it. About fourteen years ago, she burned her arm. She doesn't remember how for sure, but she thinks it was on a coffee pot or something like that. Well, she came running over to the house and she was in such a hurry that she fell up the stairs 'cause the pain was so unbearable. Her arm was all red and swollen, but it wasn't blistered yet. Granddaddy blew the fire out. Within half an hour the pain was gone and she never did get any blisters.

She remembers just how Granddaddy did it too. She described how he took her arm and made the hand motions and blew. I asked her if she heard him say anything while he was doing it and she said that he did but it was under his breath to himself.

But the folk healers do not stop with soothing burns. For every imaginable pain or malady they can provide a traditional cure. A selection of some of the more well-known ones found throughout Maryland hints at the variety of folk medicine.

For colds, rub the chest with goose grease, make a poultice of crushed onions and put it on the chest, drink kerosene and sugar.

For a cold and a cough, find a wild cherry tree, scrape off the bark; put it in a pot and boil in water. Boil it down to a syrup, add sugar and drink.

For corns, take one teaspoon of pitch, brown sugar, and saltpeter, and simmer them together. Pare the corn and place the salve on a soft piece of leather and put that over the corn. Remove it in two or three days and the corn will come off with the patch.

To cure a child of whooping cough, take him into an old mine backwards.

To get rid of freckles, wash your face in the dew of the first day of May.

To relieve a sore throat, take off the left stocking and turn it inside out and pin it around your neck.

For fertility, a man should eat sunflower seeds.

If you have a toothache, fill your mouth with water and run around the house three times without thinking about your tooth and it will go away. When this fails, run around one more time and the pain will stop for sure.

If a child has asthma, bore a hole in an upright post, put a piece of the child's hair in the hole and close it with a peg. Do this at sunrise and the asthma will go away.

To cure a child of mumps, rub his jaw on a hog trough. If he's too sick for that, bring the hog in and let him rub his jaw on the animal.

To cure an earache, blow smoke in the person's ear.

When you have a cut that won't stop bleeding, place a piece of thick rye bread on it.

My mother puts lily leaves in whiskey and when we get cut and it bleeds a lot, we wrap the lily leaf on the cut. It stops the bleeding and the cut never gets infected.

To cure athlete's foot, tie a piece of woolen yarn around the toe.

For smelly, sweaty feet, soak them several times in formaldehyde or walk barefooted as often as possible in clay.

A rattlesnake's skin around your foot eases cramps.

If you get a stye in your eye, you got it because you peed in the road. To get rid of it, rub it with an old wedding band.

Should you have a stye in either eye, go to the fork in the road and say to the first person that passes by, 'Stye, stye, leave my eye,/ Catch the first one that goes by.'

To ward off disease and keep from getting the itch, wear an asafetida bag around your neck.

To cure hiccoughs, blow into a paper bag or sip a glass of water from the opposite side, or put your index finger in your ear and drink a glass of water.

To get rid of warts, take a kernel of corn and crisscross it over the wart nine times. Then feed the corn to a chicken and the wart will go away.

Rub a wart until it bleeds; then rub the bleeding area with a flannel cloth until the bleeding stops; then bury the cloth in the ground, and when it rots the wart will go away.

Tie a knot in a string over the wart and then throw the string into the water. When the string rots, the wart will disappear.

To cure warts, find a hollow stump in the woods with water in it; wash your warts there and they will go away.

Take an old dirty penny, rub it on your warts, and then throw it over the right shoulder facing the full moon, and the wart will go away.

Rub a chicken liver over a wart; then put the liver in a holly tree in the woods and the wart will go away.

To cleanse the system, take a teaspoon of molasses and sulphur every morning in February 'til the sap rises. This is the best spring tonic I know.

A good shot of whiskey will cure anything from ingrown toenails to consumption.

Epilogue

There is a harsh and unfounded rumor abroad that folklore in Maryland is dead and that folk cultures are fast eroding with the onslaught of suburbia and the pop culture feedback of the mass media. I hope this small book has helped to convince those of that persuasion that folklore thrives. So, too, do those groups which provide it; not those groups from a hoary antiquity, but units of people bound together by some common bond, be it racial, occupational, or religious. And these groups do cry out for study.

With the recent upsurge of interest in Maryland folklore and folk culture, evidenced by the establishment of the Maryland Folklore Archive at College Park and the work of the Maryland Folklife Commission, moves are afoot to record and preserve materials from these very vital cultures. Moreover, on a larger scale, the Committee on Labor and Public Welfare has recently taken steps to place before the Congress of the United States a bill which will establish an American Folklife Foundation. This foundation, if established, will furnish funds for the study of American folk cultures and provide assistance to those attempting to bring before the public the less known arts, crafts, and lore of "grass roots" peoples.

Such activities as these, both on the state and national level, point toward optimistic ends, for they are bent on the supposition that though man has essential traits that are common, he has cultural traits that are markedly different and often embedded deep within his traditional background. Knowledge and understanding of these cultural traits can, it seems, not only expedite communication between groups, but also make the members of any one group more aware of their own cultural distinctness. Surely, time has shown that the traditions which have sprung from these cultural groups are truer and more durable than the disposable culture we confront every day on the highway, in the supermarket, or flickering across a 12/15-inch screen in our living rooms.

Footnotes

¹ For further listings, see *The Study of Folklore,* ed. Alan Dundes (Englewood, New Jersey, 1965), p. 3.

² (Philadelphia, 1968).

³ (Chicago, 1964), p. 16.

⁴ The text of this conversation, taken down on tape during the summer of 1968, can be found in the Maryland Folklore Archive under accession number (ES 70-1). Hereafter all text will simply be designated by the accession number. Those excerpts designated by a simple (H) refer to material given to the Archive by Dr. Dorothy Howard of Frostburg State College. This material, though presently the property of the Archive, has yet to be assembled and catalogued with accession numbers.

⁵ For a fine description of this design, see I. C. Peate *The Welsh House* (Liverpool, 1946), p. 93 ff.

⁶ "Legends and Tall Tales," in *Our Living Traditions,* ed. Tristram P. Coffin (New York, 1968), p. 155.

⁷ Taken from John Powell, "In the Lowlands Low," *Southern Folklore Quarterly,* I (1937), pp. 10-12.

⁸ Short items such as these appear in the Archive on 3 x 5 cards and are filed according to type.

⁹ Wayland Hand, "The Fear of God; Superstition and Popular Belief," in *Our Living Traditions*, p. 215.

¹⁰ See "Brown County Superstitions," *Midwest Folklore,* XI (1961), pp. 25-26.

Bibliography

General

Brunvand, Jan Harold, *The Study of American Folklore: An Introduction.* New York: W. W. Norton, 1968.

Coffin, Tristram P. (ed.), *Our Living Traditions.* New York: Basic Books, 1968.

Dorson, Richard M. (ed.), *Buying the Wind.* Chicago: University of Chicago, 1964. A general introduction to regional folklore in the United States.

Dundes, Alan (ed.), *The Study of Folklore.* Englewood, New Jersey: Prentice-Hall, 1965.

Glassie, Henry, *Pattern in the Material Folk Culture of the Eastern United States.* University of Pennsylvania Monographs in Folklore and Folklife No. 1. Philadelphia: University of Pennsylvania, 1968.

Gomme, Lady Alice B., *The Traditional Games of England, Scotland and Ireland.* London: D. Nutt, 1894-8.

Leach, MacEdward and Henry Glassie, *A Guide for Collectors of Oral Traditions and Folk Cultural Material in Pennsylvania.* Harrisburg: Pennsylvania Historical and Museum Commission, 1968.

Leach, Maria (ed.), *Funk & Wagnalls Standard Dictionary of Folklore, Mythology and Legend,* Two Volumes. New York: Funk & Wagnalls, 1949-50.

Yoder, Don, "The Folklife Studies Movement." *Pennsylvania Folklife,* 13:3 (July, 1963) pp. 43-56.

Maryland

Beitzell, Edwin W., *Life on the Potomac River.* Abell, Maryland: E. W. Beitzell, 1968.

Bradley, Wendell P., *They Live by the Wind.* New York: Knopf, 1969.

Brewington, M. V., *Chesapeake Bay Log Canoes and Bugeyes.* Cambridge, Maryland: Cornell Maritime Press, 1963.

Byron, Gilbert, *The Lord's Oysters.* Detroit: Gale Research Company, 1967, first published 1957. A fictionalized account but accurate portrayal of life on the Chesapeake at the beginning of the twentieth century.

Carey, George G., "Living Maryland Folklore." *Maryland English Journal*, 7:1 (Fall, 1968) pp. 1-8.

Forman, H. Chandlee, *Old Buildings, Gardens and Furniture in Tidewater Maryland*. Cambridge, Maryland: Tidewater Publishers, 1967.

Howard, Mrs. B. C., *Fifty Years in a Maryland Kitchen*. New York: M. Barrows, 1944.

Lang, Varley, *Follow the Water*. Winston-Salem, North Carolina: John F. Blair, 1961.

Middleton, Arthur P., *Tobacco Coast, A Maritime History of the Chesapeake Bay in the Colonial Era*. Newport News, Virginia: The Mariners Museum, 1953.

Mills (Howard), Dorothy (ed.), *Folk Rhymes and Jingles of Maryland Children*. Frostburg, Maryland: State Teachers College, 1944.

Tawes, Leonard S., *Coasting Captain*. Newport News, Virginia: The Mariners Museum, 1967.

Townsend, George Alfred, *Tales of the Chesapeake*. Cambridge, Maryland: Tidewater Publishers, 1968; first published 1880.

Whitney, Annie Weston and Caroline Canfield Bullock, *Folk-Lore from Maryland*. Memoirs of the American Folklore Society Vol. 28. New York: American Folklore Society, 1925.

Wolfe, Geo. W. "Hooper," *I Drove Mules on the C and O Canal*. Dover, Delaware: Woodwend Studios, 1969.

A Cook's Tour of the Eastern Shore. Compiled by Junior Auxiliary, Memorial Hospital, Easton, Maryland. Cambridge, Maryland: Tidewater Publishers, 1959.